THE
PEOPLE'S HOUSE MISCELLANY

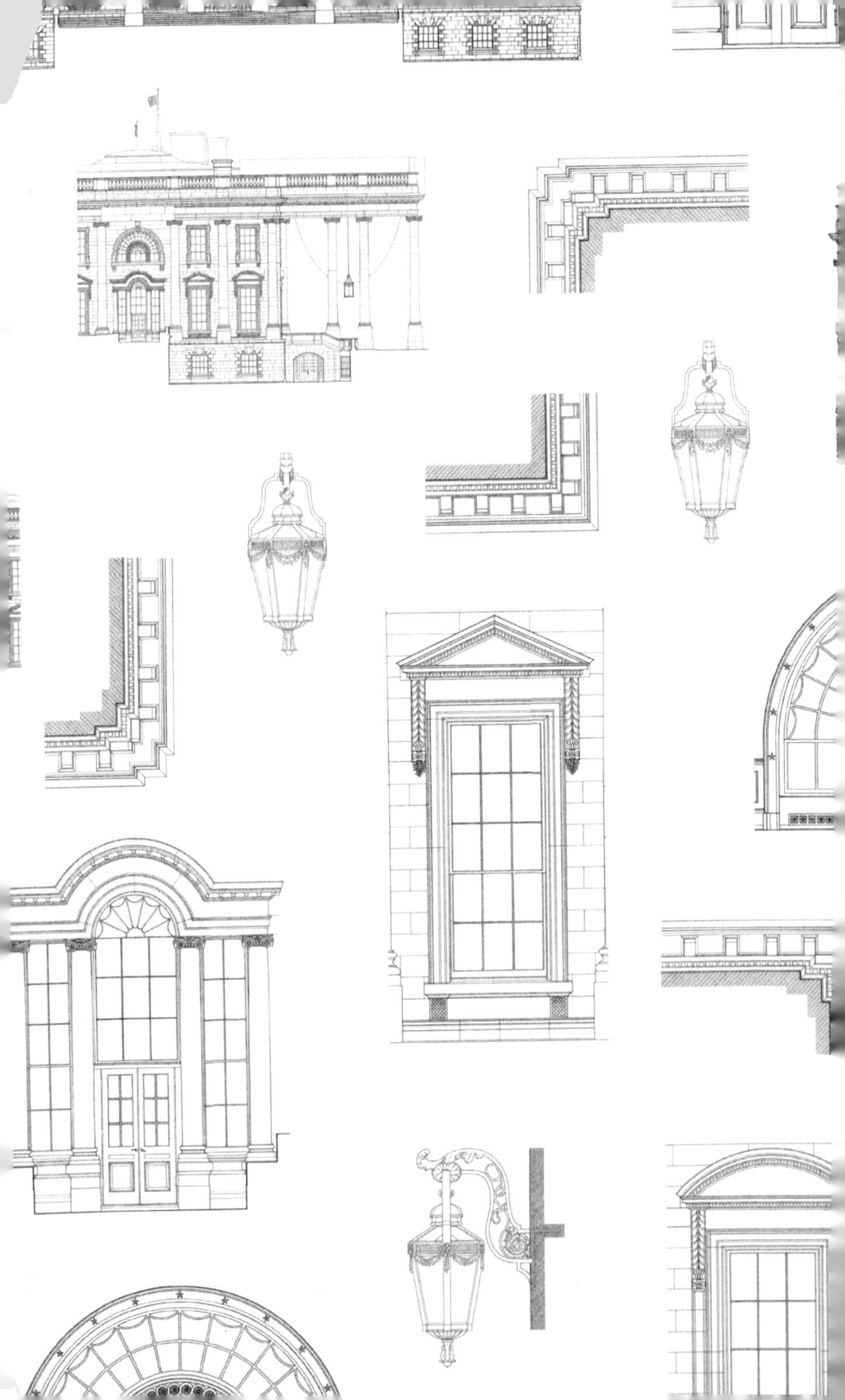

THE
PEOPLE'S HOUSE MISCELLANY

A TREASURY OF

WHITE HOUSE HISTORY, FUN FACTS,

AND

THINGS TO KNOW

BY *Stewart D. McLaurin*

THE WHITE HOUSE HISTORICAL ASSOCIATION

The White House Historical Association is a nonprofit educational association founded in 1961 for the purpose of enhancing the understanding, appreciation, and enjoyment of the Executive Mansion. All proceeds from the sale of the Association's books and products are used to fund the acquisition of historic furnishings and art work for the permanent White House Collection, assist in the preservation of public rooms, and further its educational mission.

BOARD OF DIRECTORS

John F. W. Rogers, *Chairman*
Teresa Carlson, *Vice Chairperson*
Gregory W. Wendt, *Treasurer*
Anita B. McBride, *Secretary*
Stewart D. McLaurin, *President*

Eula Adams, Gahl Hodges Burt, Merlynn Carson, Jean M. Case, Ashley B. Dabbiere, Wayne A. I. Frederick, Deneen C. Howell, Tham Kannalikham, Barbara A. Perry, Nicole Sexton, Benjamin C. Sutton Jr., Tina Tchen

National Park Service Liaison: Director of the National Park Service

Ex Officio: Archivist of the United States, Director of the National Gallery of Art, Librarian of Congress, President of the National Trust for Historic Preservation, and Secretary of the Smithsonian Institution

Directors Emeriti: John T. Behrendt, John H. Dalton, Knight Kiplinger, Elise K. Kirk, Martha Joynt Kumar, James I. McDaniel, Robert M. McGee, Ann Stock, Gail Berry West

WHITE HOUSE ENDOWMENT AND ACQUISITIONS TRUST

Frederick J. Ryan, Jr., *Chairman*
John T. Behrendt, Ashley B. Dabbiere, Anita B. McBride, James I. McDaniel, Barbara A. Perry, John F. W. Rogers, Tina Tchen

EDITORIAL AND PRODUCTION STAFF

Marcia Mallet Anderson, *Chief Publishing Officer*
Lauren McGwin, *Associate Vice President of Publishing*
Rebecca Durgin Kerr, *Editorial Director*
Jennifer Wojeck, *Editorial and Production Manager*
Mason Yang, *Research Assistant*

DESIGNER

Pentagram

Copyright © 2025 White House Historical Association.
All rights reserved under international copyright conventions. No part of this book may be reproduced or utilized in any form or by any means, electronic or mechanical, including photocopying, recording, or by any information storage and retrieval system, without permission in writing from the publisher. Unless otherwise noted, all photographs are copyrighted by the White House Historical Association. Requests for reprint permissions should be addressed to Rights and Reproductions Manager, White House Historical Association, PO Box 27624, Washington, D.C. 20038.

FIRST EDITION
10 9 8 7 6 5 4 3 2 1
Library of Congress Control Number: 2024940359
ISBN 978-1-950273-66-9
Printed in the United States of America

AUTHOR'S DEDICATION

*Dedicated to my extraordinary colleagues
of the White House Historical
Association's Publishing Department,
led by Marcia Anderson.*

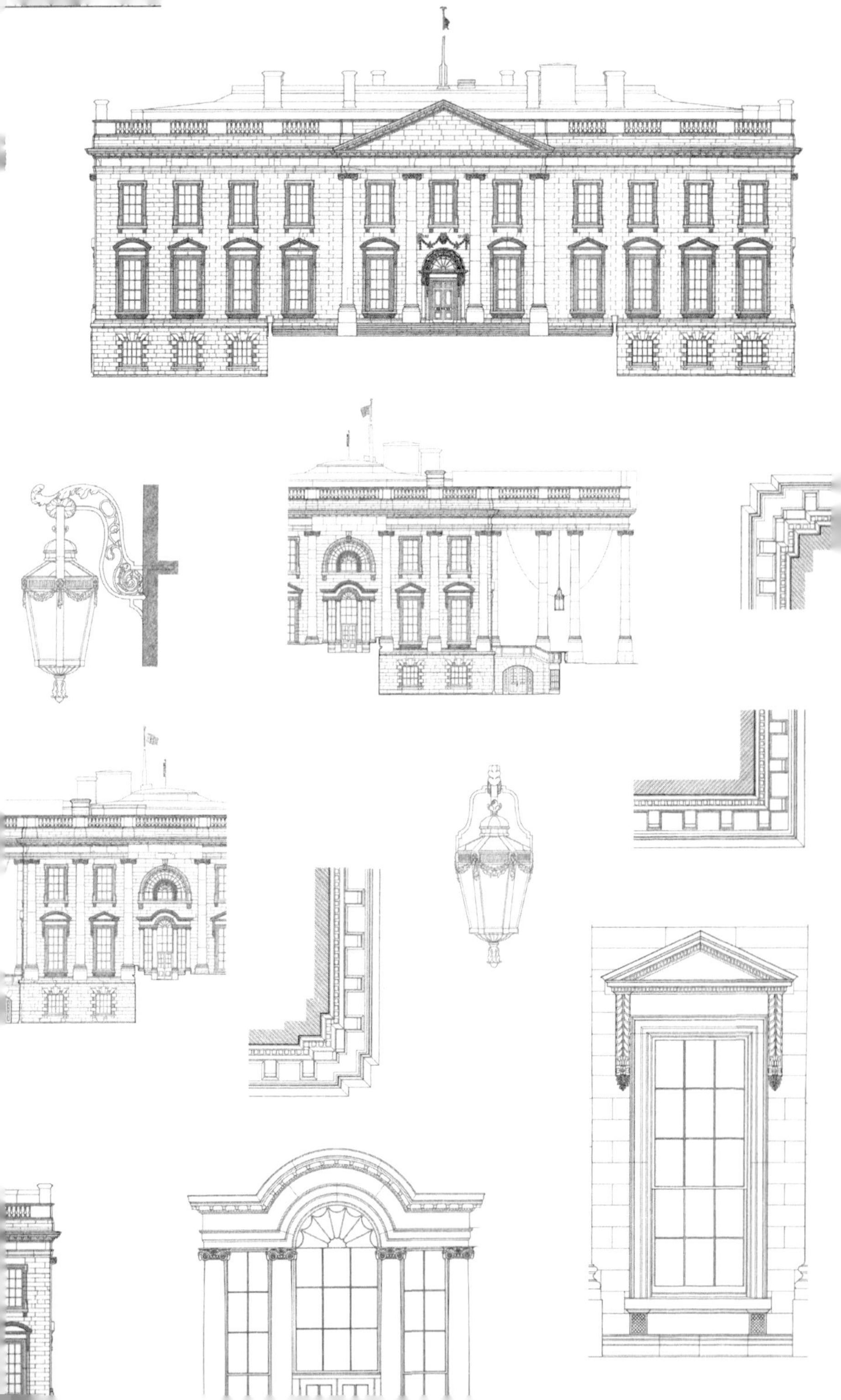

INTRODUCTION

THE HISTORY OF THE White House and those who have lived and worked there fills thousands of books and shelves in archives and libraries. It is a subject that the White House Historical Association has been devoted to sharing with the American people since 1961. From our first book *The White House: An Historic Guide*, continuously in print since 1962, to the state-of-the-art facility The People's House: A White House Experience, which opened its doors on September 23, 2024, the Association's resources alone would take years to fully explore and absorb.

"Where to begin?" is likely the first question that will be asked by those who are just starting to learn about the most famous address in America, 1600 Pennsylvania Avenue, the home and office of the president of the United States.

A great way to start building your knowledge or enriching your expertise is to delve into the facts and figures compiled on the following pages. Like the miscellany books first created in the Renaissance to entertain, this book is filled with fun facts and some surprises. There is no shortage of firsts, lasts, onlys, always, mosts, and nevers in White House history.

I hope you will find some surprises that will pique your interest and lead you on a journey to discover what interests you most about my favorite historical subject, the White House.

Stewart D. McLaurin
President
The White House Historical Association

BEFORE THE WHITE HOUSE

BEFORE THERE WAS A White House, or a Washington, D.C., the president of the United States lived in New York City and Philadelphia, the first capital cities of the United States of America.

NUMBER 3 CHERRY STREET, NEW YORK CITY

President George Washington lived in the first President's House in New York City from April 23, 1789, until February 23, 1790. The home was later converted from a residence into a commercial building and eventually demolished. The location, now under the Brooklyn Bridge, is remembered with a plaque placed on the supports of the bridge in 1899.

NUMBER 39 BROADWAY, NEW YORK CITY

President Washington lived in a second President's House on Broadway from February 23, 1790, until August 1790, when the federal government relocated to Philadelphia. The building was converted into a hotel in 1821 and demolished in the 1850s. Since 1939, the site has been occupied by the Harriman Building, which displays a plaque placed by the Daughters of the American Revolution.

MARKET STREET, PHILADELPHIA

President Washington occupied a red brick house at Sixth and Market Streets from November 27, 1790, to March 10, 1797. The third President's House was also the home of President John Adams from March 21, 1797, to May 30, 1800. The building was later used as a hotel, gutted in 1832, and completely demolished in the 1950s to make way for Independence Mall, today known as Independence National Historical Park.

Thomas J. Balcerski, "Before the White House: New York's Capital Legacy," *White House History Quarterly*, no. 69 (Spring 2023): 26–37.

A PERMANENT HOME FOR THE PRESIDENT

AN ACT FOR ESTABLISHING the Temporary and Permanent Seat of the Government of the United States, often referred to simply as the Residence Act, was signed into law by Congress on July 16, 1790. As a result of this act, the home that we know today as the White House was built.

SECTION 1 of the act calls for a new capital city to be built on the banks of the Potomac River, in an area not to exceed 10 square miles. It is the location we now know as Washington, D.C.

SECTION 3 specifies that a suitable home for the president of the United States be built in the new capital city prior to the first Monday in December of 1800. As required by the act, the President's House was built in the new city and President John Adams took residence in the house November 1, 1800.

> CHAP. XXVIII.—*An Act for establishing the temporary and permanent seat of the Government of the United States.*
>
> SECTION 1. *Be it enacted by the Senate and House of Representatives of the United States of America in Congress assembled,* That a district of territory, not exceeding ten miles square, to be located as hereafter directed on the river Potomac, at some place between the mouths of the Eastern Branch and Connogochegue, be, and the same is hereby accepted for the permanent seat of the government of the United States. *Provided nevertheless,* That the operation of the laws of the state within such district shall not be affected by this acceptance, until the time fixed for the removal of the government thereto, and until Congress shall otherwise by law provide.
>
> SEC. 2. *And be it further enacted,* That the President of the United States be authorized to appoint, and by supplying vacancies happening from refusals to act or other causes, to keep in appointment as long as may be necessary, three commissioners, who, or any two of whom, shall, under the direction of the President, survey, and by proper metes and bounds define and limit a district of territory, under the limitations above mentioned; and the district so defined, limited and located, shall be deemed the district accepted by this act, for the permanent seat of the government of the United States.
>
> SEC. 3. *And be it [further] enacted,* That the said commissioners, or any two of them, shall have power to purchase or accept such quantity of land on the eastern side of the said river, within the said district, as the President shall deem proper for the use of the United States, and according to such plans as the President shall approve, the said commissioners, or any two of them, shall, prior to the first Monday in December, in the year one thousand eight hundred, provide suitable buildings for the accommodation of Congress, and of the President, and for the public offices of the government of the United States.
>
> SEC. 4. *And be it [further] enacted,* That for defraying the expense of such purchases and buildings, the President of the United States be authorized and requested to accept grants of money.
>
> SEC. 5. *And be it [further] enacted,* That prior to the first Monday in December next, all offices attached to the seat of the government of the United States, shall be removed to, and until the said first Monday in December, in the year one thousand eight hundred, shall remain at the city of Philadelphia, in the state of Pennsylvania, at which place the session of Congress next ensuing the present shall be held.
>
> SEC. 6. *And be it [further] enacted,* That on the said first Monday in December, in the year one thousand eight hundred, the seat of the government of the United States shall, by virtue of this act, be transferred to the district and place aforesaid. And all offices attached to the said seat of government, shall accordingly be removed thereto by their respective holders, and shall, after the said day, cease to be exercised elsewhere; and that the necessary expense of such removal shall be defrayed out of the duties on imposts and tonnage, of which a sufficient sum is hereby appropriated.
>
> APPROVED, July 16, 1790.

The Residence Act.

THE WHITE HOUSE IS BUILT AND EVOLVES

1792	President George Washington approves the design made by James Hoban for the President's House.
1792	The cornerstone is set.
1798	The exterior Aquia sandstone walls are completed and whitewashed.
1800	President John Adams moves into the President's House.
1814	Invading British troops burn the President's House to its stone walls during the War of 1812.
1818	The reconstructed President's House is opened with a public reception.
1824	The South Portico is added.
1829–30	The North Portico is built.
1835	The first of many greenhouses is built on the South Grounds.
1901	The name of the President's House officially becomes the White House.
1902	A major renovation is undertaken during Theodore Roosevelt's presidency. The greenhouse complex is replaced with the West Wing to house offices for presidential staff, and the East Wing is built.
1909	The West Wing is doubled in size to include the Oval Office for the use of the president of the United States.
1927	The attic is converted into the Third Floor with guest rooms and the Solarium.
1929	The West Wing is gutted by fire.

THE WHITE HOUSE IS BUILT AND EVOLVES

1934	The size of the West Wing is tripled, and the Oval Office is moved to its present location adjacent to the Rose Garden.
1942	The East Wing is rebuilt as a two-story structure.
1947–48	The Truman Balcony is added to the South Portico.
1948–52	A second major renovation is undertaken during the Truman presidency. The interior of the White House is completely reconstructed within the historic stone shell.
1969	The Children's Garden is created on the South Grounds.
1970	A columned porch is added to the entrance of the West Wing.
1975	An outdoor swimming pool and cabana are built.
1980–96	The exterior stone walls are stripped of nearly forty layers of paint, cleaned, and conserved.
1992	A time capsule is buried on the grounds to mark the 200th anniversary of the laying of the cornerstone.
2000	The 200th anniversary of the White House as the home of the presidents is celebrated.
2020	The Tennis Pavilion is erected on the South Grounds.

JAMES HOBAN'S WINNING DESIGN

IN MARCH OF 1792, the Commissioners of the City of Washington launched a competition for the design of the President's House. It was President George Washington who chose the design by the Irishman James Hoban as the winner.

JAMES HOBAN'S LIFE AND WORK

1755	Born in County Kilkenny, Ireland
1770s	Attends the Dublin Society School of Architectural Drawing in Dublin, Ireland
1780	Is awarded the prestigious silver medal for "Drawings of Brackets, Stairs, Roofs &c." by the Dublin Society
1770–85	Gains building experience in Dublin through work on the Royal Exchange, the Newcomen Bank, and the Custom House
1785	Immigrates to Philadelphia, Pennsylvania
1787	Relocates to Charleston, South Carolina
1790	Establishes school of architectural drawing in Charleston
1791	Becomes known by reputation to President George Washington during his visit to Charleston
1792	Is named winner of the architectural design competition for the President's House
1793	Is a founding member and first Master of Washington's first Freemason Lodge, Federal Lodge No. 1
1793–1800	Oversees construction of the President's House
1793–1810	Builds Blodgett's Hotel on the block of E and F, 7th and 8th Streets, NW., destroyed by fire in 1836
1794	Helps found St. Patrick's, the first Roman Catholic Church, in the Federal District
1799	Contributes to the design of John Tayloe's Octagon House

JAMES HOBAN'S LIFE AND WORK

1802	Founds the Society of the Sons of Erin, which helped Irish workers who needed housing, food, and medicine.
1806	Builds St. Mary's Chapel near Capitol Hill
1809	Constructs a larger building for St. Patrick's
1814	Is appointed to supervise the rebuilding of the President's House after it was burned by the British
1815	Expands St. Patrick's Church and adds the Washington Catholic Seminary building
1820	Contributes to the founding of Washington City's second Catholic church, St. Peter's
1824	Builds the South Portico for President James Monore
1829–30	Builds the North Portico for President Andrew Jackson
1831	Died and was buried in Holmstead's Burying Ground
1863	Reinterred at Mount Olivet Cemetery

Stewart D. McLaurin, *James Hoban: Designer and Builder of the White House* (Washington, D.C.: White House Historical Association, 2021).

ENSLAVED LABORERS AND THE WHITE HOUSE

BUILDING THE PRESIDENT'S HOUSE

Much of the labor to build the President's House was performed by enslaved men of African descent. Many of these workers were hired from property owners in Maryland and Virginia. Among their many roles were quarrying and hauling stone, felling trees, sawing timbers, and making bricks.

HOUSEHOLD WORKERS

Today most members of the White House household staff are salaried federal employees who hold their jobs from one presidency to the next, but the early presidents were responsible for the costs of running the house, including the wages of the servants. John and Abigail Adams, the first White House residents, brought their own servants with them to the house in 1800. Nine of the presidents who followed before the Civil War either brought enslaved workers with them or relied on enslaved labor at the White House. These presidents included Thomas Jefferson, James Madison, James Monroe, John Quincy Adams, Andrew Jackson, Martin Van Buren, John Tyler, James K. Polk, and Zachary Taylor.

Betty C. Monkman, *Life in the White House* (Washington, D.C.: White House Historical Association, 2023).

THE NORTH DOOR AND GREAT SWAG

PRESIDENT WASHINGTON TOOK SPECIAL DELIGHT in fine stonework and enjoyed the dramatic effect of light and shadow upon both the smooth walls and intricate carvings. It is an effect enhanced by the traditional white paint. The climax of the fine stone masonry is the garland and swag of leaves, acorns, flowers, and fierce griffins that crown the main entrance. The draped festoon was hand-carved about 1796. Several forms of iron chisels were used to cut into the faces of two great Aquia stones, which, when finished, were hoisted with pulleys and rope to their present location and mortared together side by side, 14 feet across.

William Seale, *A White House of Stone* (Washington, D.C.: White House Historical Association, 2017): 90.

THE DOUBLE SCOTTISH ROSE

THE DOUBLE SCOTTISH ROSE, propagated in Scotland in the 1780s, was adopted by the Scots stonemasons as a motif for the columns and other parts of the White House. Introduced by them in about 1796 on the heroic pilasters of the east and west ends of the house, the device was repeated in the portico columns of 1824 and 1829–30.

William Seale, *A White House of Stone* (Washington, D.C.: White House Historical Association, 2017): 92.

THE NAME OF THE HOME AND OFFICE OF
THE PRESIDENT OF THE UNITED STATES

President's House
Used to refer to the first presidential homes in New York
and Philadelphia and to mark the site of the house
on the 1792 Plan of the City of Washington made by
Pierre Charles L'Enfant. This term is still used unofficially today.

Presidential Palace
An unofficial reference sometimes used in the
early nineteenth century.

Presidential Mansion
An unofficial reference sometimes used in the
early nineteenth century.

Executive Mansion
The official name of the building from 1840 to 1901.

White House
Used informally throughout the nineteenth century to reference
the color of the house, the White House was made the
official name of the house in 1901 by President Theodore Roosevelt.

People's House
A reference made by Jacqueline Kennedy and incorporated
in the name of The People's House: A White House Experience
at 1700 Pennsylvania Avenue NW, Washington, D.C.

JOHN ADAMS MOVES IN

JUNE 30, 1800 — President John Adams inspects the President's House, still under construction in the City of Washington.

NOVEMBER 1, 1800 — John Adams, the second president of the United States, becomes the first president to live in the President's House.

NOVEMBER 2, 1800 — John Adams writes to his wife Abigail, reporting his arrival and his wish for her company. He ends the letter with his now famous prayer, asking heaven to bestow the best of blessings on the house.

NOVEMBER 16, 1800 — Abigail Adams arrives in the City of Washington and joins her husband at the President's House.

JANUARY 1, 1801 — President and Mrs. Adams host the first New Year's Day reception at the President's House, beginning a tradition that will last for more than a century.

FEBRUARY 17, 1801 — Thomas Jefferson is certified as the winner of the presidential election of 1800. Adams had come in third and in December knew he had lost reelection.

MARCH 4, 1801 — John Adams departs the President's House at 4:00 a.m. and does not attend Thomas Jefferson's Inauguration.

NOVEMBER 1, 2000 — The two-hundredth anniversary of the President's House is celebrated with a re-enactment of the arrival of President Adams by horse-drawn carriage. The president's descendants are in attendance.

LETTER FROM JOHN ADAMS TO ABIGAIL ADAMS

ONE DAY AFTER PRESIDENT JOHN ADAMS moved into the new President's House, he wrote to his wife, Abigail, who would soon join him. He chose not to describe the house in his letter so that she could form her own opinion, but he did write what has become a famous prayer for the future of the house. The prayer is now engraved in the mantel in the State Dining Room of the White House.

———————— WASHINGTON, NOVEMBER 2, 1800 ————————

My Dearest Friend,

We arrived here last night, or rather yesterday, at one o Clock and here we dined and Slept. The Building is in a State to be habitable. And now we wish for your Company....

I shall say nothing of public affairs. I am very glad you consented to come on, for you would have been more anxious at Quincy than here, and I, to all my other Solicitudines Mordaces as Horace calls them i.e. "biting Cares" should have added a great deal on your Account. Besides it is fit and proper that you and I should retire together and not one before the other.

Before I end my Letter I pray Heaven to bestow the best of Blessings on this House and all that shall hereafter inhabit it. May none but honest and wise Men ever rule under this roof.

I shall not attempt a description of it. You will form the best Idea of it from Inspection....

I am with unabated Confidence and affection your
John Adams

John Adams to Abigail Adams, November 2, 1800. *Adams Family Papers: An Electronic Archive*, Massachusetts Historical Society website, www.masshist.org.

LETTER FROM ABIGAIL ADAMS TO HER DAUGHTER

WHEN FIRST LADY ABIGAIL ADAMS arrived at the President's House on November 16, 1800, the grounds surrounding the house were yet to be landscaped and remained a muddy construction site, but she saw the promise of the future in the bleak scene she encountered.

In a letter written to her daughter, Abigail Adams Smith, on November 21, 1800, Abigail Adams describes her new home and voiced a number of complaints, but she was optimistic. "It is a beautiful spot, capable of every improvement," she wrote.

———————— WASHINGTON, NOVEMBER 21, 1800 ————————

My Dear Child,

I arrived here on Sunday last, and without meeting with any accident worth noticing, except losing ourselves when we left Baltimore.... woods are all you see, from Baltimore until you reach the city, which is only so in name. The river, which runs up to Alexandria, is in full view of my window, and I see the vessels as they pass and repass. The house is upon a grand and superb scale, requiring about thirty servants to attend and keep the apartments in proper order, and perform the ordinary business of the house and stables; an establishment very well proportioned to the President's salary. The lighting the apartments, from the kitchen to parlours and chambers, is a tax indeed; and the fires we are obliged to keep to secure us from daily agues is another very cheering comfort....

The house is made habitable, but there is not a single apartment finished, and all withinside, except the plastering, has been done since Briesler came. We have not the least fence, yard, or other convenience, without, and the great unfinished audience-room I make a drying-room of, to hang up the clothes in. The principal stairs are not up, and will not be this winter.... Up stairs there is the oval room, which is designed for the drawingroom, and has the crimson furniture in it. It is a very handsome room now; but, when completed, it will be beautiful.... It is a beautiful spot, capable of every improvement, and, the more I view it, the more I am delighted with it.

Letter from Abigail Adams to Abigail Adams Smith, November 21, 1800. *Founders Online*, National Archives website, www.founders.archives.gov.

THE WHITE HOUSE IS OLD AND YET . . . .

The White House is old by our standards and yet it is young. I can count nearly fifty years—a quarter of the total life of the White House of walking up the Northwest Drive in the constant pursuit of news, more of which is funneled through the White House than any other place.

And like almost everyone who works in or around the White House for any time at all, I have come to view the building as an enduring and comforting friend in times of tragedy and as a counselor of caution in moments of national euphoria.

It always whispers to me, "Nothing is as good as it may seem right now—and nothing is as bad as you may judge in the moment."—Hugh Sidey

---

Hugh Sidey, Introduction to *The White House Remembered: Recollections by Presidents Richard M. Nixon, Gerald R. Ford, Jimmy Carter, and Ronald Reagan,* ed. Hugh Sidey (Washington, D.C.: White House Historical Association, 2005), 15.

THE WHITE HOUSE BY THE NUMBERS

Street address . . . . 1600 PENNSYLVANIA AVENUE NORTHWEST
Zip code 20500

Latitude 38.897957
Longitude . . . . −77.036560
Elevation above sea level[1] . . . . 69 FEET

Zone on the USDA Hardiness scale 7A
Average summer temperature . . . . 85°F
Average winter temperature . . . . 40°F

Acreage of the White House Grounds . . . . 18.84 ACRES

Total square footage[2] . . . . 99,800 SQUARE FEET
Length from east to west of the Residence[3] . . . . 168 FEET
Width from north to south[4] . . . . 152 FEET
Height of South Front . . . . 70 FEET
Height of North Front . . . . 60 FEET 4 INCHES

NUMBER OF

Floors 6
Rooms 132
Doors 412
Windows 147
Bathrooms 35
Fireplaces 28
Staircases 8
Kitchens 4
Elevators 3

---

1. Approximate measurement
2. Including the East and West Wings
3. Not including the East and West Wings
4. Including the porticoes

DOES THE WHITE HOUSE HAVE

... a swimming pool?

Yes — President Franklin D. Roosevelt had an indoor swimming pool built in the West Terrace in 1933. During the Nixon administration, the Press Briefing Room was built over the pool. President Gerald R. Ford had an outdoor swimming pool built on the South Lawn in 1975, where it remains today.

... a tennis court?

Yes — Built in 1902 behind the executive offices, the tennis court was later moved to the west side of the South Lawn to make room for expanding the executive offices in 1909, including the new Oval Office. President Barack Obama modified the present-day tennis court to allow for both tennis and basketball.

... a helicopter landing pad?

No — *Marine One*, the presidential helicopter, lands on the South Lawn of the White House not on a constructed landing pad. Before the arrival of *Marine One*, large red temporary disks are placed on the South Lawn to facilitate a smooth landing.

... a bowling alley?

Yes — First built in 1947 in the West Wing basement, the bowling lanes were relocated to the Old Executive Office Building in 1955. President Richard Nixon, a bowling enthusiast, installed a single lane in 1969 underneath the North Portico driveway.

... a library?

Yes — The White House Library is decorated with early American antiques and furniture and is located on the Ground Floor. Originally used as a laundry room and later a waiting room for male guests, the space was converted into the Library in 1935.

... a horse stable?

Not anymore — From 1806 to 1909, the White House did have a series of stables. In 1909, the last stable, built in 1872, was converted into an automobile garage before ultimately being torn down in 1911.

... a movie theater?

Yes — President Franklin D. Roosevelt converted an East Terrace cloakroom into the Movie Theater in 1942. Although renovated since, the space still functions as a theater, which seats forty-six viewers.

WHITE HOUSE OVALS

——— BLUE ROOM ———
State Floor · This room is situated directly opposite the North Door, and is 40 feet long with an 18-foot ceiling · The striking vista through the South Portico makes it the principal drawing room in the White House · This room has been known as the Blue Room since Martin Van Buren's redecoration of 1837, which changed it from crimson red.

——— DIPLOMATIC RECEPTION ROOM ———
Ground Floor · This room is situated directly beneath the Blue Room · This room was where the first permanent furnace was installed in 1837 and served as a furnace room until 1902, when President Theodore Roosevelt converted the room into a formal entrance and reception room for visiting dignitaries and members of the Washington Diplomatic Corps · It is the principal entrance for the first family and their personal guests · President Franklin D. Roosevelt's fireside chats usually took place in this room, reaching millions of Americans in a friendly, conversational manner by which the president simplified the complexities of his solutions to the Depression and calmed the nation's fears.

——— YELLOW OVAL ROOM ———
Second Floor · During the Hayes presidency, this room was used as a library · The family would gather here for their weekly hymn-singing session while Secretary of the Interior Carl Schurz played the piano · As part of First Lady Jacqueline Kennedy's restoration project, the Yellow Oval Room was made into a formal drawing room for the Private Quarters · The yellow scheme was chosen by Mrs. Kennedy to echo the yellow damask furnishings and curtains selected by Dolley Madison when this room was the Ladies' Drawing Room.

——— OVAL OFFICE ———
West Wing · This iconic room used as the president's office was created in 1909 for William Howard Taft · The shape was modeled after the three oval rooms in the White House and has been in its current location since 1934, when Franklin D. Roosevelt expanded the West Wing.

THE GARDENS BY THE NUMBERS

1
Japanese maple tree planted by
First Lady Frances Folsom Cleveland is still standing.

4
mature saucer magnolias were transplanted from the
Tidal Basin into President John F. Kennedy's redesigned
Rose Garden in 1962.

9
weeping cherry trees were planted by First Lady Lady
Bird Johnson around the fountain on the South Grounds.

18
Japanese cherry trees were planted by First Lady
Helen Herron Taft near the fountain basin on the South Lawn.

51
varieties of plants were grown in
President James Madison's White House garden.

489
trees were growing on the White House Grounds during
Theodore Roosevelt's presidency.

MORE THAN 700
saplings were planted by President John Quincy Adams.

30,000
summer annuals were planted during
Benjamin Harrison's presidency.

63,250
flowering spring bulbs were planted by First Lady
Frances Folsom Cleveland on the White House Grounds.

EVOLUTION OF THE WHITE HOUSE FENCE

Circa 1801	A post and rail fence was built around the White House. At the southern end of the South Lawn, an 8-foot stone wall was built to keep livestock off the South Grounds.
1818–19	A semicircular driveway with eight stone piers and an iron fence was built across the North Front.
1833	A wrought iron fence was built on top of the stone wall across of the North Front.
1902	The Jackson-era North Portico railing was replaced by a parapet wall.
1937	The wrought-iron fence surrounding the South Lawn was replaced by a steel fence affixed with pointed bronze tips.
1941	The grounds were closed, limiting access to only those with appointments. Gatehouses were built at the perimeter.
1976	The nineteenth-century gates at the North Drive were replaced with steel gates to withstand automobile crashes.
1995	Pennsylvania Avenue, between 17th and 15th Streets, was closed to vehicle traffic.
2004	With the assistance of landscape architects and security personnel, construction was completed on a newly designed Pennsylvania Avenue in front of the White House to accommodate both pedestrian traffic and enhanced security measures.
2015	Removable metal points were installed on top of the White House fence as a temporary measure to deter climbing and fence jumping.
2019–24	The 6 foot 6 inch tall fence was replaced by a new steel fence with a height of nearly 13 feet. The wider and stronger fence posts feature anticlimb and intrusion detection technology.

THE ONLY PRESIDENT

... to never live in the White House:
   George Washington

... to learn English as a second language:
   Martin Van Buren

... to also serve as Speaker of the House:
   James K. Polk

... to also serve as Chief Justice of the United States:
   William Howard Taft

... to be ordained:
   James A. Garfield

... who was never married:
   James Buchanan

... to get married in the White House:
   Grover Cleveland

... now buried in Washington, D.C.:
   Woodrow Wilson

... born on the Fourth of July:
   Calvin Coolidge

... elected to serve four terms:
   Franklin D. Roosevelt

... to live more than 100 years:
   Jimmy Carter

... to attend a Super Bowl game in person:
   Donald J. Trump

THE FIRST FIRST LADY

... to serve as first lady:
    Martha Washington

... to live in the White House:
    Abigail Adams

... to attend an Inaugural Ball:
    Dolley Madison

... to earn a college degree:
    Lucy Hayes

... to teach college classes while serving as first lady:
    Jill Biden

... to get married in the White House:
    Frances Cleveland

... to travel as first lady outside of the United States with her husband:
    Edith Roosevelt

... to cast a vote for president of the United States:
    Florence Harding

... to run for president of the United States:
    Hillary Clinton

... to have an office in the East Wing:
    Rosalynn Carter

... to break a Guinness World Record:
    Michelle Obama

... to add art by an Asian American artist to the White House Collection:
    Melania Trump

Anita McBride and Giovanna McBride, *First Ladies Make History* (Washington, D.C.: White House Historical Association, 2024).

THE TRUMAN BALCONY: A BEAUTIFUL VIEW

*I did not oppose Truman when he put in the balcony.
We used the Truman Balcony all the time. I had too many problems
with Congress to care about a balcony. Things should be
done to the White House for utilitarian purposes.*
—PRESIDENT RICHARD M. NIXON

---

*Betty and I liked the Truman Balcony. We would go out there
on a pleasant night for a wonderful panoramic view of Washington.
From there, we could sit and watch the city and the monuments.*
—PRESIDENT GERALD R. FORD

---

*For the Truman Balcony, we imported six rocking chairs from Georgia.
I would quite often meet up with my staff members and cabinet officers
there, and sometimes foreign visitors would come up and spend an
afternoon with us. Many times after a state banquet, we'd go up and talk
while looking over the Washington Monument, the Jefferson Memorial,
and the National Airport. It is a very enjoyable place.*
—PRESIDENT JIMMY CARTER

---

*I think that every president since Harry Truman must have given
a prayer of thanks for what he did in refurbishing the White House.
One of the major things he did was build a balcony out
from the residence area. At the time, he was criticized severely for it,
but one can stand there now and look out over the South Lawn
for a beautiful view. In the warm summer weather,
I'd go upstairs for lunch out on the balcony. I always liked that.*
—PRESIDENT RONALD REAGAN

Hugh Sidey, ed. *The White House Remembered: Recollections by Presidents Richard M. Nixon, Gerald R. Ford, Jimmy Carter, and Ronald Reagan* (Washington, D.C.: White House Historical Association, 2005), 45, 51–52, 69, 82.

INAUGURAL FIRSTS

1789
George Washington takes the first Oath of Office in New York City.

1793
George Washington is the first to take the Oath of Office in Philadelphia and the first to take the oath on March 4.

1801
Thomas Jefferson is the first to take the Oath of Office in the City of Washington.

1817
James Monroe is the first to take the Oath of Office in an outdoor ceremony at the U.S. Capitol.

1825
John Quincy Adams is the first son of a former president to take the Oath of Office.

1829
Andrew Jackson is the first to take the Oath of Office on the East Front of the Capitol.

1861
President Abraham Lincoln is the first to take the Oath of Office wearing a Brooks Brothers suit.

1877
Rutherford B. Hayes is the first to take the Oath of Office in the Red Room.

1909
William Howard Taft is the first to take the Oath of Office inside the Capitol when a blizzard forces the outdoor ceremony to be canceled.

1937
Franklin D. Roosevelt is the first to take the Oath of Office on January 20.

1945
Franklin D. Roosevelt is the first to take the Oath of Office on the South Portico of the White House.

1945
Harry S. Truman is the first to take the Oath of Office in the Cabinet Room.

1963
Lyndon B. Johnson is the first to take the Oath of Office on *Air Force One*.

1974
Gerald R. Ford is the first to take the Oath of Office in the East Room.

1977
Jimmy Carter is the first to exit his motorcade to walk from Capitol Hill to the White House.

1981
Ronald Reagan is the first to take the Oath of Office on the West Front of the Capitol.

2009
Barack Obama is the first Black man to take the Oath of Office.

2013
Barack Obama is the first to take the Oath of Office in the Blue Room.

THE WHITE HOUSE
FINE AND DECORATIVE ARTS COLLECTION

MORE THAN 50,000
pieces of furniture, lighting fixtures, rugs, china, glassware, and flatware.

1,575
French and English gilded silver (vermeil) objects.

MORE THAN 500
paintings, sculptures, and drawings.

MORE THAN 500
pieces from the five-course State Dinner and Dessert Service made for President and Mrs. Hayes featuring unusual shapes and designs of flora and fauna created by Theodore Russell Davis.

NEARLY 200
paintings donated by the White House Historical Association.

21
chandeliers.

6
paintings by Albert Bierstadt.

2
Steinway pianos.

1
desk presented by Queen Victoria to President Hayes made from the timbers of the British ship HMS *Resolute*.

"THERE SHALL BE IN THE WHITE HOUSE A CURATOR OF THE WHITE HOUSE"

EXECUTIVE ORDER 11145 of March 7, 1964, provides that "There shall be in the White House a Curator of the White House." The order specifies that "The Curator shall assist in the preservation and protection of the articles of furniture, fixtures, and decorative objects used or displayed in the principal corridor on the ground floor and the principal public rooms on the first floor of the White House, and in such other areas in the White House as the President may designate." As of April 2025, nine individuals have served in the role.

Curator of the White House	Years Active
Lorraine W. Pearce	1961–1962
William Voss Elder	1962–1963
James R. Ketchum	1963–1970
Clement E. Conger	1970–1986
Rex W. Scouten	1986–1997
Betty C. Monkman	1997–2002
William G. Allman	2002–2017
Lydia S. Tederick	2017–2023
Donna Hayashi Smith	2024–

Betty C. Monkman, "There Shall Be in the White House a Curator of the White House," *White House History Quarterly*, no. 56 (Winter 2020): 86–93.

COLLECTION FIRSTS

First	Title	Date	Artist/Author
First book on an artwork painted in the White House	*Six Months at the White House with Abraham Lincoln: The Story of a Picture*	1866	Francis Bicknell Carpenter
First seascape added to the collection	*A Summer Day at Salisbury Beach*	1890	James Henry Moser
First painting of the White House added to the collection	*Our White House, Washington, D.C.*	1942	Anita Willets-Burnham
First American Impressionist painting added to the collection	*The Avenue in the Rain*	1963	Childe Hassam
First book on official White House china	*Official White House China*	1975	Margaret Brown Klapthor
First book on White House glassware	*White House Glassware: Two Centuries of Presidential Entertaining*	1989	Jane Shadel Spillman
First book on the White House fine arts collection	*Art in the White House*	1992	William Kloss

COLLECTION FIRSTS

First painting by an American folk artist added to the collection	*The President's House*	1992	Rufus Porter
First painting by a Black artist added to the collection	*Sand Dunes at Sunset*	1995	Henry Ossawa Tanner
First book on the White House decorative arts collection	*The White House: Its Historic Furnishings and First Families*	2000	Betty Monkman
First White House furnishings exhibition catalog	*Something of Splendor*	2011	William Allman and Melissa Naulin
First painting by a Black woman added to the collection	*Resurrection*	2014	Alma Thomas
First paintings by a Pop Artist added to the collection	*Water Lilies—Pink Flower* and *Water Lilies—Blue Lily Pads*	2016	Roy Lichtenstein
First artwork by an Asian American artist added to the collection	*Floor Frame*	2020	Isamu Noguchi
First book co-written by four White House curators	*Furnishing the White House: The Decorative Arts Collection*	2023	Betty C. Monkman, William Allman, Lydia Tederick, and Melissa Naulin

SAVED: WASHINGTON'S PORTRAIT

COMPLETED IN 1797, Gilbert Stuart's painting of George Washington was the first piece of artwork purchased for display in the White House.

On August 24, 1814, during the War of 1812, British troops invaded Washington, D.C. After it became known that British soldiers were only miles away, Dolley Madison and several servants rescued what they could. Seeing Stuart's painting of President Washington in the Dining Room, Mrs. Madison ordered it saved, and it was carried off to a safe hiding place in Maryland. Later that night, the White House was gutted by the fire set by British troops. The famous portrait survived and currently hangs in the East Room of the White House.

William Seale, *The Night They Burned the White House: The Story of Tom Freeman's Painting* (Washington, D.C.: White House Historical Association, 2014).

SAVED: RED VELVET CURTAINS

THE OVAL ROOM (now the Blue Room) during the Madison presidency was richly adorned to impress the visitors during the many receptions and levees held there. A focal point of the room was the red velvet drapery, made in Georgetown by Mary Sweeney, that hung on the south-facing windows. Loved by Dolley Madison, but considered gaudy by Benjamin Henry Latrobe, the curtain fabric was all he could procure in large yardage on short notice. A red velvet ball gown belonging to Dolley Madison and preserved in the Greensboro Historical Museum collection is believed to have been made from the red velvet curtains she saved from the White House ahead of the fire in 1814.

Conover Hunt, "Getting It Right: The Embellished Obligations of Dolley Madison," *White House History*, no. 35 (Summer 2014): 8–17.

LOST: CHAIRS BY LATROBE

BENJAMIN HENRY LATROBE was commissioned by President James Madison to design furnishings for the Oval Drawing Room (now the Blue Room) in 1809. Inspired by Grecian forms made fashionable in London, Latrobe adapted the Greek klismos form for the chairs with stretchers added between the legs for strength. The painted suite, made by the Baltimore firm of Hugh and John Finlay, was destroyed in the 1814 fire, but Latrobe's design drawings still survive in the Maryland Center for History and Culture in Baltimore, Maryland.

William Seale, "The White House Before the Fire," *White House History*, no. 4 (Fall 1998): 22.

RETURNED: MEDICINE CHEST

BELIEVED TO HAVE BELONGED to President James Madison and looted by British troops before they set fire to the White House during the War of 1812, this medicine chest ended up with British officer Thomas Kains, paymaster of the HMS *Devastation*. His grandson presented it to President Franklin D. Roosevelt in 1939, at a time when the president was planning to build a museum in the White House. It was later removed to Hyde Park with the president's personal effects until it was lent to the White House by the Roosevelt Library in 1961. The medicine chest became a permanent part of the White House Collection in 2012.

William G. Allman, "The White House Collection: Reminders of 1814, A New Look for the Bicentennial," *White House History*, no. 35 (Summer 2014): 52.

TELEVISION IN THE WHITE HOUSE

OCTOBER 5, 1947
President Harry S. Truman gave the first televised speech from the White House. He was the first president to allow television cameras inside the White House.

MAY 3, 1952
President Harry S. Truman led a televised tour of the newly rebuilt White House. It was broadcast by ABC, NBC, and CBS to a small audience of early television owners.

FEBRUARY 14, 1962
First Lady Jacqueline Kennedy led a televised tour of the White House. Eighty million viewers tuned in to the documentary entitled *A Tour of the White House with Mrs. John F. Kennedy*, which was produced by CBS News.

JULY 20, 1969
President Richard M. Nixon watched the Apollo 11 mission on two television sets in the Oval Office, one pulled toward the desk and the other closer to the wall. As he watched, he was also televised making a call to the astronauts from the White House to the moon.

MAY 26, 1970
First Daughter Tricia Nixon led the first televised tour of the Private Quarters on the Second Floor of the White House for CBS.

FEBRUARY 2, 1977
President Jimmy Carter televised a fireside chat from the White House Library.

"The White House and Television" *White House History Quarterly*, no. 67 (Fall 2022): entire issue.

PRESIDENT JOHN F. KENNEDY ON TOURING THE WHITE HOUSE

PRESIDENT JOHN F. KENNEDY joined the televised tour led by First Lady Jacqueline Kennedy near the end of the program on February 14, 1962. This page.transcribed from his notes for the segment, includes his observation that a tour of the White House reminds visitors that the presidents were real people who "ate and slept and worked and suffered."

Mr. President, what do you think of the changes that have taken place in the White House?

Well, as you can see, the White House is really becoming a panorama of American history -- it is the story of American civilization on display. I am proud of the things my wife has done to bring out the historical aspects of this Mansion and to remind us of the richness of this legacy.

You don't mind the visitors?

No -- I am all for them. We have about 1.3 million visitors a year -- and a good many of them, I am always glad to see are young people. I think it is very important for young people to visit the house where every President since John Adams has lived and where the great decisions of our history have been made. History sometimes seems to be too much a study of abstractions and phantoms. A visit to the White House reminds us all that these were real people, our Presidents; that they ate and slept and worked and suffered; and that they met their responsibilities with all the courage and wisdom they could muster.

Mary Jo Binker, "Jacqueline Kennedy's Televised Tour of the White House," *White House History Quarterly*, no. 67 (Fall 2022): 80. Transcribed notes are from the John F. Kennedy Presidential Library and Museum.

RESPECTS PAID IN THE EAST ROOM

SEVEN PRESIDENTS HAVE lain in state in the East Room following their deaths while in office.

William Henry Harrison
APRIL 7, 1841

Zachary Taylor
JULY 13, 1850

Abraham Lincoln
APRIL 18, 1865

William McKinley
SEPTEMBER 16, 1901

Warren G. Harding
AUGUST 7–8, 1923

Franklin D. Roosevelt
APRIL 14, 1945

John F. Kennedy
NOVEMBER 23, 1963

KNOWN DEATHS OF FIRST FAMILY MEMBERS IN THE WHITE HOUSE

EIGHT PRESIDENTIAL FAMILY MEMBERS are known to have died in the President's House.

APRIL 4, 1841
President William Henry Harrison

SEPTEMBER 10, 1842
First Lady Letitia Tyler

JULY 9, 1850
President Zachary Taylor

FEBRUARY 20, 1862
President Abraham Lincoln's Son
William ("Willie") Wallace Lincoln

DECEMBER 15, 1873
First Lady Julia Grant's Father
Frederick Dent

OCTOBER 25, 1892
First Lady Caroline Scott Harrison

AUGUST 6, 1914
First Lady Ellen Axson Wilson

DECEMBER 5, 1952
First Lady Bess Truman's Mother
Margaret Gates Wallace

WEDDINGS AT THE WHITE HOUSE

President Grover Cleveland became the first president to be married in the White House on June 2, 1886, when he wed Frances Folsom.

WEDDINGS AT THE WHITE HOUSE

ONE PRESIDENT and numerous presidential family members are among those who have married in the White House.

Date	Couple	Location
MARCH 29, 1812	Lucy Payne Washington to Thomas Todd	BLUE ROOM*
MARCH 9, 1820	Maria Monroe to Samuel Laurence Gouverneur	BLUE ROOM*
FEBRUARY 25, 1828	John Adams to Mary Catherine Hellen	BLUE ROOM
APRIL 10, 1832	Mary A. Eastin to Lucius J. Polk	EAST ROOM
JANUARY 31, 1842	Elizabeth Tyler to William Waller	EAST ROOM
MAY 21, 1874	Nellie Grant to Algernon Sartoris	EAST ROOM
JUNE 19, 1878	Emily Platt to Russell Hastings	BLUE ROOM
JUNE 2, 1886	President Grover Cleveland to Frances Folsom	BLUE ROOM
FEBRUARY 17, 1906	Alice Roosevelt to Nicholas Longworth III	EAST ROOM
NOVEMBER 25, 1913	Jessie Wilson to Francis Bowes Sayre	EAST ROOM
MAY 7, 1914	Eleanor Wilson to William Gibbs McAdoo	BLUE ROOM
AUGUST 7, 1918	Alice Wilson to Isaac Stuart McElroy Jr.	BLUE ROOM
DECEMBER 9, 1967	Lynda Johnson to Charles Robb	EAST ROOM
JUNE 12, 1971	Tricia Nixon to Edward Cox	ROSE GARDEN
MAY 28, 1994	Anthony Rodham to Nicole Boxer	ROSE GARDEN
NOVEMBER 19, 2022	Naomi Biden to Peter Neal	SOUTH LAWN

*Most likely location

LYNDA JOHNSON'S WEDDING CAKE

ON DECEMBER 9, 1967, Lynda Bird Johnson, the eldest daughter of President Lyndon B. Johnson, married Captain Charles S. Robb in the East Room of the White House. The recipe for her wedding cake, shared by White House Executive Chef Henry Haller in his book *The White House Family Cookbook*, makes two 9 × 5-inch loaves or two 9-inch layers.

3 sticks (1½ cups) butter, softened

2 cups confectioners' sugar

8 eggs, at room temperature

3 cups plus 3 tablespoons sifted cake flour

¼ teaspoon ground mace

1 lemon rind, finely grated

1. Preheat oven to 325°F. Lightly grease two 9 × 5-inch loaf pans or two 9-inch layer pans.
2. In a large mixing bowl, cream butter until light and fluffy.
3. Gradually add sugar and beat well.
4. Add eggs one at a time, beating after each addition.
5. Mix in flour, mace, and lemon rind and blend until smooth.
6. Divide batter between prepared pans and bake on lower shelf for 50 minutes, or until toothpick inserted in center comes out clean. (After 15 minutes, loaves can be split with a sharp knife to allow air to escape; make a clean slit ¼-inch deep and 6 inches in length along the top of each loaf.) Turn out of pans and cool on wire racks before icing.

Henry Haller with Virginia Aronson, *The White House Family Cookbook* (Washington, D.C.: White House Historical Association, 2023): 63.

TRICIA NIXON'S WEDDING CAKE

ON JUNE 12, 1971, Tricia Nixon, the eldest daughter of President Richard M. Nixon, married Edward Cox in the White House Rose Garden. The recipe for her wedding cake, shared by White House Executive Chef Henry Haller in his book *The White House Family Cookbook*, makes one 6-layer, 8-inch cake, or two 3-layer cakes.

2 sticks (1 cup) unsalted butter

2 cups sugar

1 cup milk

10 egg whites, at room temperature

4 teaspoons baking powder

4 cups sifted flour

1 teaspoon almond extract

1. Preheat oven to 350°F. Grease six 8-inch layer pans; dust with flour.
2. In a large mixing bowl, cream butter with sugar until very light and smooth.
3. Add milk a little at a time; beat well after each addition.
4. In a clean, dry bowl, beat egg whites until stiff.
5. Sift baking powder with flour; add to batter alternately with stiff egg whites, folding well after each addition. Fold in almond extract.
6. Pour into prepared pans and bake for 25 minutes, or until toothpick inserted in center comes out clean. Turn out and let cake cool completely on wire racks before frosting.

Henry Haller with Virginia Aronson, *The White House Family Cookbook* (Washington, D.C.: White House Historical Association, 2023): 145.

LONGEST SERVING
WHITE HOUSE STEWARDS AND CHIEF USHERS

WHO	STEWARD						CHIEF USHER				
	Jean-Pierre Sioussat	Antoine Michel Giusta	Joseph Boulanger	Valentino Melah	William Sinclair	Henry Pinckney	Thomas E. Stone	Irwin ("Ike") Hoover	Howell G. Crim	J. B. West	Rex W. Scouten	Gary Walters
PERIOD	1809–1817	1825–1833	1833–1845	1869–1877	1885–1901	1901–1909	1903–1911	1913–1933	1938–1957	1957–1969	1969–1986	1986–2007

IKE HOOVER

IRWIN HOOD ("IKE") HOOVER was an employee of the Edison Company when he was sent to the White House on May 6, 1891, during Benjamin Harrison's presidency, to install the first electric lights at the house. He remained on the staff as an electrician until he was promoted to a position in the Usher's Office. In 1913 he was named chief usher, a position he held until his death in 1933. During his forty-two years of service he served ten presidents. His memoir, *Forty-Two Years in the White House*, was published in 1934 after his death. In the following excerpt, he recalls his assignment to install electricity at the White House:

——— I BECOME, LIKE THE ELECTRIC LIGHTS, A PERMANENT FIXTURE ———

In due time I got down to the job of wiring and installing the electric appliances. The wonderful old chandeliers, built for gas, were converted into combination fixtures and the candle wall brackets were replaced by electric fixtures in the fashion of the time. While working through the house, necessarily going into every room, we often ran across the Harrison family.

The Harrisons were all much interested in this new and unusual device that was being installed; so much so, that we got quite well acquainted with them. They gave us much encouragement, and it was a genuine pleasure to be thus surrounded while doing what was, at best, a hard job. By the fifteenth of September, a little over four months after we began, the job was finished, the current turned on, and the White House illuminated with electric lights for the whole world to behold.

Irwin Hood ("Ike") Hoover, *Forty-Two Years in the White House*, 10th ed. (Cambridge, Mass.: Riverside Press, 1939): 6.

FIRST STATE DINNER VISITS

1874 — Sandwich Islands (Hawaii)	1959 — Argentina El Salvador Ireland Soviet Union	1977 — Bahamas Barbados Bolivia Chile
1931 — France Thailand	1960 — Japan Nepal	Costa Rica Dominican Republic
1933 — Panama	1961 — India Pakistan Peru Sudan Tunisia	Grenada Guatemala Guyana Honduras
1939 — United Kingdom		
1941 — Luxembourg		
1942 — Colombia Cuba		Jamaica
1943 — Haiti Paraguay	1962 — Ivory Coast Saudi Arabia	Nigeria Suriname
1944 — Iceland Poland Venezuela	1963 — Afghanistan Morocco	Tanzania Trinidad and Tobago
	1964 — Israel	
	1965 — Upper Volta	Uruguay
1945 — Canada	1966 — Senegal	1979 — China
1947 — Mexico	1968 — Burma Kuwait Norway	1980 — Kenya
1949 — Belgium Brazil Denmark Italy Iran Netherlands Philippines Portugal		1983 — Bahrain Oman
	1969 — Australia Jordan Laos New Zealand Sierra Leone	1984 — Sri Lanka
		1985 — Algeria
		1987 — Sweden
		1988 — Mali
	1970 — DR Congo Finland Indonesia	1990 — Yemen
		1992 — Germany Russia
1951 — Ecuador		
1953 — Greece		1994 — South Africa
1954 — Ethiopia Liberia South Korea Turkey	1971 — Yugoslavia	1999 — Ghana Hungary
	1973 — Romania Singapore	
	1974 — Austria	
	1975 — Egypt Zambia	
1957 — South Vietnam		
1958 — West Germany	1976 — Spain	

As of May 2025. Names of countries are given as they were at the time of the dinner.

THE PEOPLE'S HOUSE MISCELLANY

STATE DINNERS:
PRESIDENTS WHO HOSTED THE MOST

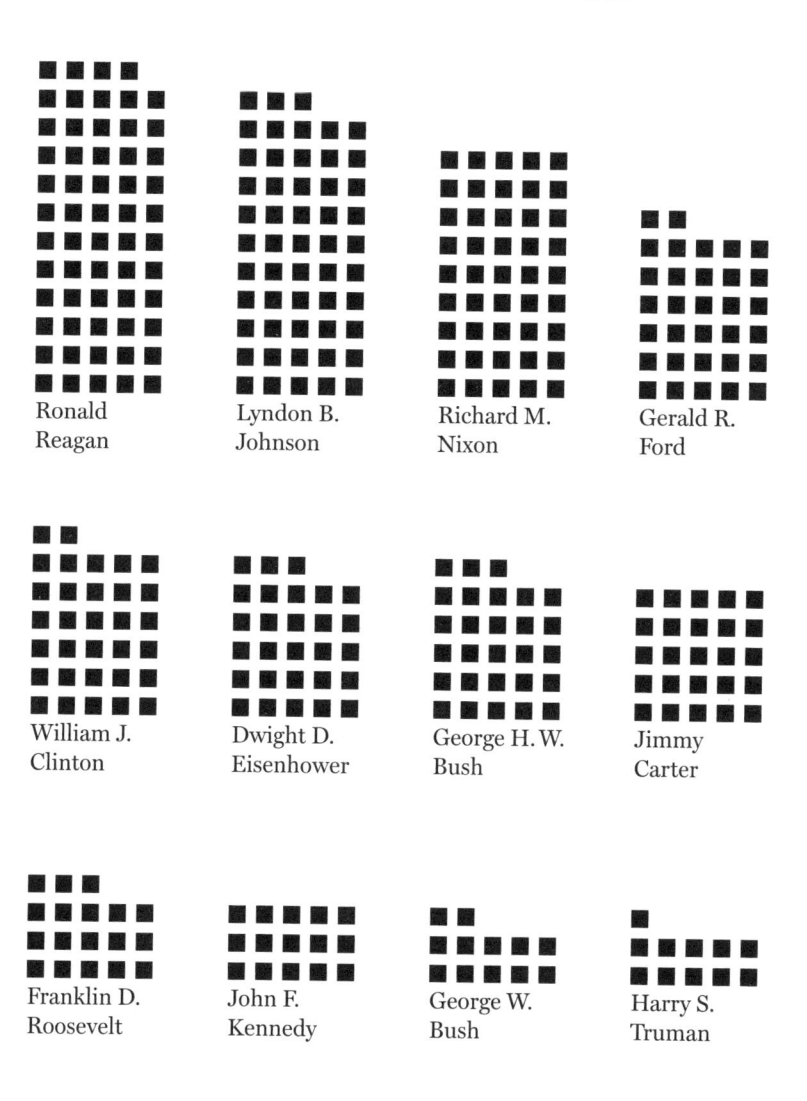

Ronald Reagan

Lyndon B. Johnson

Richard M. Nixon

Gerald R. Ford

William J. Clinton

Dwight D. Eisenhower

George H. W. Bush

Jimmy Carter

Franklin D. Roosevelt

John F. Kennedy

George W. Bush

Harry S. Truman

As of May 2025. Only State Dinners given for foreign heads of state and heads of government are included.

THE PEOPLE'S HOUSE MISCELLANY

WINE AND THE WHITE HOUSE

DINNER

Inglenook Pinot Chardonnay

Aspic of salmon Dorian
Sauce Vincent

Château Haut-Brion 1955

Roast spring lamb
Rice à l'Orientale
Spinach à la crème

Green Salad
Brie Cheese

Piper Heidsieck 1955

Bombe glacé aux pêches
Petits-fours sec

The White House
Monday, June 3, 1963

JUNE 3, 1963 An Inglenook Pinot Chardonnay from California and a 1955 Château Haut-Brion are included on the menu for a dinner hosted by President and Mrs. John F. Kennedy honoring President Sarvepalli Radhakrishnan of India. The Kennedys served the first California wine, an Almaden Pinot Noir, at a State Dinner on September 19, 1961, in honor of President Manuel Prado Ugarteche of Peru.

Frederick J. Ryan, Jr. *Wine and the White House: A History* (Washington, D.C.: White House Historical Association, 2020), 271, 298.

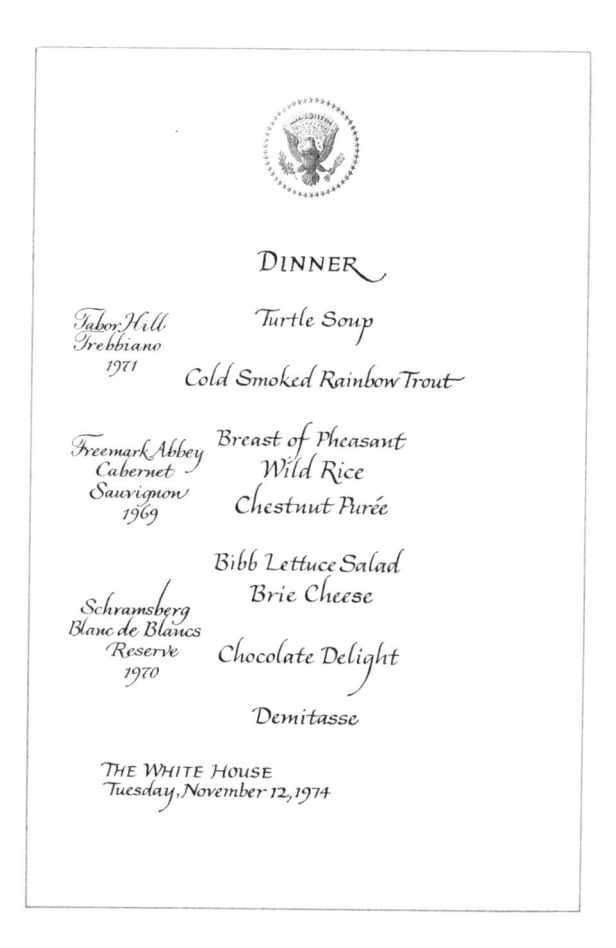

WINE AND THE WHITE HOUSE

> **DINNER**
>
> Tabor Hill Trebbiano 1971
>
> Turtle Soup
>
> Cold Smoked Rainbow Trout
>
> Freemark Abbey Cabernet Sauvignon 1969
>
> Breast of Pheasant
> Wild Rice
> Chestnut Purée
>
> Bibb Lettuce Salad
> Brie Cheese
>
> Schramsberg Blanc de Blancs Reserve 1970
>
> Chocolate Delight
>
> Demitasse
>
> THE WHITE HOUSE
> Tuesday, November 12, 1974

NOVEMBER 12, 1974 Marking both the first time a White House menu included a wine from a sitting president's home state and a wine from the Midwest, Tabor Hill Vidal Blanc (mistakenly identified as Trebbiano on the menu) from Michigan was selected by President Gerald R. Ford for a dinner held in honor of Chancellor Bruno Kreisky of Austria.

Frederick J. Ryan, Jr. *Wine and the White House: A History* (Washington, D.C.: White House Historical Association, 2020), 78, 320.

WINE AND THE WHITE HOUSE

DINNER

Poached Halibut in Dill Sauce
Fleurons

Sliced Tenderloin of Beef
Sauce Choron
Soufflé Potatoes
Broiled Tiny Tomatoes
Artichokes St. Germain

Bibb Lettuce Salad
Brie Cheese

Chestnut Bombe
Acorn Petits Fours

Château Montelena
Chardonnay 1979
Jordan
Cabernet Sauvignon 1976
Schramsberg
Crémant Demi-sec 1979

THE WHITE HOUSE
Monday, November 2, 1981

NOVEMBER 2, 1981 Only California wines were served at President and Mrs. Reagan's State Dinner honoring King Hussein I of Jordan, including Chateau Montelena Chardonnay 1979, Jordan Cabernet Sauvignon 1976, and Schramsberg Crémant Demi-sec 1979. Jordan was a newly launched wine that became a favorite of President Reagan. The 1973 vintage of the Chateau Montelena had famously finished first in the historic Judgment of Paris five years earlier.

Frederick J. Ryan, Jr. *Wine and the White House: A History* (Washington, D.C.: White House Historical Association, 2020), 158 159, 332.

> ### DINNER
> *Honoring*
> The Governors of the States and Territories
>
> Maine Lobster with Carrot Soup
> Infused Risotto
> *Llano Estacado Cellar Select Chardonnay 1999 (Texas)*
>
> Grilled Yearling Beef with Truffled Potatoes
> Roasted Onions and Herbed Vegetable Ragout
> *Rex Hill "Jacob Hart" Pinot Noir 1998 (Oregon)*
>
> Winter Greens with Maytag Bleu Cheese in Brioche
> Sherry Dressing
>
> Chocolate Tumbleweed
> Honey Parfait
> Poached Pear in Pomegranate Sauce
> *Linden Vineyards Late Harvest 1999 (Virginia)*
>
> **THE WHITE HOUSE**
> Sunday, February 25, 2001

FEBRUARY 25, 2001 White House guests were introduced to the geographically diverse fine wines of the United States at President Bush's dinner for the Governors of the States and Territories. The menu lists Llano Estacado Cellar Select Chardonnay 1999 from Texas, Rex Hill Jacob Hart Pinot Noir 1998 from Oregon, and Linden Vineyards Late Harvest 1999 dessert wine from Virginia.

Frederick J. Ryan, Jr. *Wine and the White House: A History* (Washington, D.C.: White House Historical Association, 2020): 373.

"HAIL TO THE CHIEF": NOTABLE WHITE HOUSE MUSICAL EVENTS

Date	Performer	Event
January 1, 1801	The Marine Band	First performance at the White House
1861–65 (Civil War)	The Marine Band	Weekly concerts on the White House Grounds and in the adjacent Lafayette Park[1]
November 13, 1878	Marie ("Selika") Williams	First Black opera singer to perform at the White House[2]
April 22, 1889	The Marine Band conducted by John Philip Sousa	First performed at the White House Easter Egg Roll
November 15, 1911	Mormon Tabernacle Choir	Performed for President and Mrs. William Howard Taft in the East Room
June 8, 1939	Marian Anderson	Sang at the White House during a visit from King George VI and Queen Elizabeth of England[3]
November 13, 1963	Bagpipers from The Black Watch (Royal Highland Regiment) of Scotland	Performed on the South Lawn[4]
April 29, 1969	Duke Ellington	Performed at the White House on his 70th birthday and received the Presidential Medal of Freedom
	President Richard Nixon	Played "Happy Birthday" on the piano

"HAIL TO THE CHIEF": NOTABLE WHITE HOUSE MUSICAL EVENTS

June 18, 1978	James Hubert ("Eubie") Blake and Dizzy Gillespie	Jazz festival on the South Lawn, hosted by President Jimmy Carter
1981–89	A broad variety of artists including Johnny Mathis, Liza Minnelli, and Patti Austin	"In Performance at the White House," a televised concert series[5]
June 18, 1993	President William J. Clinton	Played saxophone on stage along with musicians on the South Lawn[6]
November 24, 2014	Stevie Wonder	President Barack Obama awarded the Presidential Medal of Freedom to the singer-songwriter[7]
2017–21	Washington National Opera, the "President's Own" United States Marine Chamber Orchestra, and other military bands[8]	Various performances at the Trump White House
June 12, 2023	Audra McDonald, Jennifer Hudson, and Cliff ("Method Man") Smith	Juneteenth concert on the South Lawn, hosted by President Joe Biden[9]

(1) To raise morale in wartime Washington, D.C. (2) Williams sang her program for President and Mrs. Hayes in the Green Room. (3) Nearly two months after her famous performance at the Lincoln Memorial. (4) Members of this band would play again less than two weeks later at President John F. Kennedy's funeral. (5) Launched in 1978 featuring classical music, which grew during the Reagan administration. (6) In celebration of the fortieth anniversary of the Newport Jazz Festival. Clinton told the audience of 400 that "Jazz is really America's classical music. Like our country itself and especially the people who created it, jazz is a music of struggle, but played in celebration." (7) Obama told the audience that Wonder's 1972 album *Talking Book* was the first album he bought with his own money. (8) Including the United States Army Herald Trumpets, the United States Navy Band Sea Chanters, and the United States Air Force Strings. (9) Two years prior, June 19th was signed into law as a federal holiday.

STATE CHINA ORDERS

AS THE GUEST LISTS for State Dinners increased, so too did the need for more place settings. The following list includes the approximate number of pieces ordered for State China Services over time:

PRESIDENT	NUMBER OF PIECES
James Monroe	479
Franklin Pierce	287
Abraham Lincoln	190
Ulysses S. Grant	587
Rutherford B. Hayes	562
Benjamin Harrison	444
Theodore Roosevelt	1,764
Woodrow Wilson	1,422
Franklin D. Roosevelt	1,722
Harry S. Truman	1,572
Lyndon B. Johnson	2,208
Ronald Reagan	4,370
Bill Clinton	3,600
George W. Bush	4,480
Barack Obama	3,520

William G. Allman, *Official White House China from the 18th to the 21st Centuries*, 2nd ed. (Washington, D.C.: White House Historical Association, 2016).

A PRESIDENT'S CHINA ON THE TABLE

Whenever we had an exchange of conflicting ideas or views, which our family has always had at mealtimes, we would be sobered by the fact that we would always have a different president's china on the table. We would think of the lives of those who had used them: Adams and Jefferson, Lincoln, Jackson, and Wilson, and many others. It was a constant daily reminder that we were sharing with them the history of a great country.
—President Jimmy Carter

Quoted in Hugh Sidey, ed., *The White House Remembered: Recollections by Presidents Richard M. Nixon, Gerald R. Ford, Jimmy Carter, and Ronald Reagan* (Washington, D.C.: White House Historical Association, 2005), 67–68.

YEAR WHEN WHITE HOUSE CHRISTMAS TREES WERE FIRST SUPPLIED FROM EACH STATE

1961
Massachusetts

1963
Vermont

1965
West Virginia

1966
Wisconsin

1967
Ohio

1968
Indiana

1971
North Carolina

1972
Washington

1974
Michigan

1975
New York

1981
Pennsylvania

1991
Oregon

1994
Missouri

TYPES OF BLUE ROOM CHRISTMAS TREES

FIRS

SPRUCES

PINES

FIRST LADY JACQUELINE KENNEDY established the tradition of displaying a thematically decorated Christmas tree in the Blue Room in 1961. As of Christmas 2015, the tradition has been interrupted only twice. In 1962, the tree was displayed in the Entrance Hall instead of the Blue Room because of renovation work. In 1969, First Lady Pat Nixon chose the Entrance Hall again to make the tree more visible. More than fifty of these trees have been firs but on occasion, spruces and pines have been selected.

THE OFFICIAL WHITE HOUSE CHRISTMAS ORNAMENT: A BELOVED TRADITION

EACH YEAR FOR MORE than forty years, the White House Historical Association has produced a new ornament specially designed to commemorate a presidency or to mark an anniversary in the history of the White House. Millions of these ornaments now decorate Christmas trees in the United States and abroad, and many have been hung on trees in the White House itself.

1981
Angel in Flight

1982
Dove of Peace
George Washington

1983
The North Front
John Adams

1984
Peace Medal
Thomas Jefferson

1985
Madison Silhouettes
James Madison

1986
The South Portico
James Monroe

1987
White House Doors
John Quincy Adams

1988
The Children
Andrew Jackson

1989
The Presidential Seal
200th Anniversary
of the Presidency

1990
The Blue Room
Martin Van Buren

1991
A White Charger
William H. Harrison

1992
The White House
200th Anniversary
of the White House
Cornerstone

1993
*Portrait of First Lady
Julia Gardiner Tyler*
John Tyler

1994
*United States
Marine Band*
James K. Polk

1995
Patriotic Christmas
Zachary Taylor

1996
First Presidential Seal
Millard Fillmore

1997
*White House
Renovations*
Franklin Pierce

1998
*The American
Bald Eagle and Shield*
James Buchanan

1999
*Portrait of President
Abraham Lincoln*
Abraham Lincoln

2000
*The North and
South Fronts*
200th Anniversary of
the White House

2001
*A First Family's
Carriage Ride*
Andrew Johnson

THE OFFICIAL WHITE HOUSE CHRISTMAS ORNAMENT: A BELOVED TRADITION

2002
The South Front
Centennial of the
Roosevelt Renovation

2003
*A Child's Rocking
Horse*
Ulysses S. Grant

2004
*A First Family's
Sleigh Ride*
Rutherford B. Hayes

2005
The South Front
James A. Garfield

2006
*Tiffany Glass in the
White House*
Chester A. Arthur

2007
A President Marries
Grover Cleveland

2008
*A Victorian
Christmas Tree*
Benjamin Harrison

2009
*The First
Christmas Tree with
Electric Lights*
Grover Cleveland

2010
*The Army and
Navy Reception*
William McKinley

2011
Santa Visits
Theodore Roosevelt

2012
*The First Presidential
Automobile*
William H. Taft

2013
North Lawn Elm Tree
Woodrow Wilson

2014
Presidential Special
Warren Harding

2015
*The National
Christmas Tree*
Calvin Coolidge

2016
*The Christmas Eve
Fire of 1929*
Herbert Hoover

2017
*The Bald Eagle,
Inaugural Cartouche*
Franklin D. Roosevelt

2018
The Truman Balcony
Harry S. Truman

2019
*The First Presidential
Helicopter*
Dwight D. Eisenhower

2020
*Portrait of President
John F. Kennedy*
John F. Kennedy

2021
*Blue Room
Christmas Tree*
Lyndon B. Johnson

2022
*The White House
in Gingerbread*
Richard M. Nixon

2023
Holiday Wreath
Gerald R. Ford

2024
*The Anchor:
A Symbol of Hope*
Jimmy Carter

2025
*Presidential
Diplomacy*
150th Anniversary
of State Dinners

2026
America's 250

CHEF ROLAND MESNIER'S
WHITE HOUSE GINGERBREAD HOUSES

CHEF ROLAND MESNIER oversaw the construction of more than a dozen White House gingerbread houses during his time as a pastry chef at the White House, from 1979 to 2004. The tradition of making a gingerbread house for display in the State Dining Room began with Chef Hans Raffert's German A-frame style houses in 1969 and continues today with houses made of white chocolate by Pastry Chef Susie Morrison. But Mesnier was famous for his enormous and ambitious thematic creations and shared the story of his designs in his book *The White House in Gingerbread*.

1992 *The American Christmas Village*	1996 *The Nutcracker*	2001 *Home for the Holidays*
1993 *The House of Socks*	1997 *Santa's Workshop*	2002 *All Creatures Great & Small*
1994 *The President's Boyhood Home*	1998 *The Wonderland Castle*	2003 *A Storybook White House*
1995 *The First Lady's Childhood Home*	1999 *Treasures of the Nation's Capital*	2004 *The Red & White Gingerbread House*
	2000 *Christmases of the Clinton White House Past*	

Roland Mesnier with Mark Ramsdell, *The White House in Gingerbread* (Washington, D.C.: White House Historical Association, 2015). Chef Mesnier's trademark signature is pictured above.

CHEF ROLAND MESNIER'S WHITE HOUSE EGGNOG

CHEF MESNIER recalled that "many White House guests who didn't think they liked eggnog enjoyed this recipe immensely."

Serves 12

1 quart cold heavy cream
10 pasteurized egg yolks (it is important to use pasteurized, not raw, eggs)
10 large egg whites
2 tablespoons superfine sugar
⅓ cup granulated sugar
1½ cups blended whiskey
¾ cup dark Jamaican rum
2 cups cold milk
¾ cup heavy syrup
Grated rind of 1 orange
Grated rind of 1 lemon
Ground nutmeg

1. Place the cold heavy cream in a 2 gallon punch bowl. Fold together the whipped yolks, whipped heavy cream, and whipped egg whites, and beat by hand until the cream doubles in volume and holds soft peaks.
2. In a separate bowl, whip the yolks on high speed until they are light and very thick.
3. Place the egg whites in the bowl of an electric mixer fitted with the whisk attachment. With the mixer on high, add the ⅓ cup granulated sugar and whip the egg whites until they hold very soft peaks.
4. Pour the foamy egg whites into the whipped yolks and mix until they are thoroughly combined.
5. Slowly stir in the heavy syrup, whiskey, dark rum, and cold milk.
6. Sprinkle the top of the eggnog with the orange zest, lemon zest, and grated nutmeg.
7. Place the punch bowl in the refrigerator and chill for at least 4 hours or overnight. The eggnog will thicken as it chills.

Roland Mesnier with Mark Ramsdell, *The White House in Gingerbread* (Washington, D.C.: White House Historical Association, 2015), 160.

THE WHITE HOUSE EASTER EGG ROLL

Following a tradition that began in 1878, the president and first lady welcome children and their families onto the White House Grounds to celebrate Easter Monday with a fun-filled day that is now one of the oldest, and most popular, annual events in the history of the White House. The lucky guests gather to roll brightly dyed hard-boiled eggs down the sloped South Lawn, and over the years other activities—games, music, story-time, and dancing to name only a few—have been added to ensure that everyone has a good time.

1860s–1870s

Presidents Andrew Johnson and Ulysses S. Grant are said to have hosted the first White House Egg Rolls in the 1860s and 1870s, but they were small gatherings limited to family and close friends.

1878

President Rutherford B. Hayes invited youngsters to come and roll their eggs at the White House. The annual White House Easter Egg Roll had officially begun.

1889

President Benjamin Harrison added live music to the Easter Egg Roll. With his two-year-old grandson, he stepped onto the South Portico just as the U.S. Marine Band struck up a rousing march. The band performed all day for the children's entertainment and continues to provide entertaining music for the Egg Roll to this day.

1905

During Theodore Roosevelt's presidency attendance at the Easter Egg Roll grew so huge that in 1905, adults were banned unless accompanied by a child. But those denied entry simply resorted to "borrowing" children from outside the gates, and opportunistic kids quickly realized they could earn some pocket money from the change in policy.

1917–1920

President Woodrow Wilson followed the tradition until 1917, when America's entry into World War I forced the event to be moved to the Washington Monument Grounds, for safety concerns. Food rationing stopped the Egg Roll from 1918 through 1920.

THE WHITE HOUSE EASTER EGG ROLL TIMELINE

1921
President Warren G. Harding and his wife, First Lady Florence Harding, took great pleasure in resuming the annual White House Easter Egg Roll in 1921.

1933–1945
From 1933 to 1941, Franklin Delano Roosevelt presided over nine White House Easter Egg Rolls, more than any other president. Following U.S. entry into World War II in December 1941, the Easter Egg Roll was moved from the White House Grounds to the Capitol Grounds. But it was not to last. Wartime security measures completely shut down the festivities from 1943 to 1945.

1953
After a twelve-year lapse, President Dwight D. Eisenhower revived the customary White House Easter Egg Roll on April 6, 1953.

1981
First Lady Nancy Reagan introduced a hunt for wooden eggs that bore the signatures of famous people. The eggs are now designed to reflect the unique theme of each year's event and feature the signatures of the president and first lady.

2009
Since 2009 during the presidency of Barack Obama, tickets to the White House Easter Egg Roll have been distributed via an online lottery, allowing people from across the United States an equal chance to attend in person.

2020–2022
COVID-19 forced the cancellation of the White House Easter Egg Roll from 2020 through 2021. The Egg Roll returned in 2022 during the presidency of Joe Biden.

2025
The first Egg Roll of the second term of President Donald Trump saw the return of real hard-boiled and colored eggs in place of plastic eggs for use in activities on the South Lawn.

Jonathan Pliska, *The White House Easter Egg Roll: A History for All Ages* (Washington, D.C.: White House Historical Association, 2018). Illustration by John Hutton.

"MANY FIRST FAMILIES HAVE LOVED THIS HOUSE"

THE FIRST EDITION OF *The White House: An Historic Guide* went on sale July 4, 1962, to a public eager to learn more about the history of the White House and its Public Rooms. The first project of the White House Historical Association, the historic guide has remained continuously in print for more than sixty years, with more than 10 million copies sold. It was First Lady Jacqueline Kennedy's wish that such a book be written, and her letter opened the first edition. Since that time eleven first ladies have continued the tradition of sharing an opening message to the guide. Here are some of the things they said:

————— JACQUELINE KENNEDY, 1ST EDITION, 1962 —————
"Many First Families loved this house ... and each and every one left something of themselves behind in it."

————— LADY BIRD JOHNSON, 5TH EDITION, 1964 —————
"Its rooms, its furniture, its paintings, its countless mementos make it a living story of the whole experience of the American people."

————— PAT NIXON, 9TH EDITION, 1970 —————
"We love this house because it lives and grows—as does the Nation.... This is your heritage. This is your house."

————— BETTY FORD, 12TH EDITION, 1975 —————
"It has been the living symbol of America and the home of the First Families since 1800."

————— ROSALYNN CARTER, 13TH EDITION, 1977 —————
"There is nothing here that does not have a human story behind it or that is not part of our nation's fascinating history."

————— NANCY REAGAN, 15TH EDITION, 1982 —————
"This wonderful, historic house symbolizes the continuity of our democracy from generation to generation."

"MANY FIRST FAMILIES HAVE LOVED THIS HOUSE"

BARBARA BUSH, 17TH EDITION, 1991
"It is your house, and we know you appreciate and treasure it as much as we do."

HILLARY RODHAM CLINTON, 18TH EDITION, 1994
"Each work of art, each highly polished antique, every carefully restored architectural detail speaks to us of the families who have preceded us in this residence."

LAURA BUSH, 21ST EDITION, 2001
"The White House is a masterwork in progress, crafted by the American heroes who lived and worked here and cherished by those who lay claim to it—the people of the United States."

MICHELLE OBAMA, 23RD EDITION, 2011
"From bill signings to State Dinners to Easter Egg Rolls, this house serves as a backdrop to our national memory. Every day, a part of the American story unfolds here at the White House."

MELANIA TRUMP, 24TH EDITION, 2017
"My sincere hope is that these images will also give way to thoughts of the many families and children who have called the White House home, a place of refuge, rest, and inspiration."

JILL BIDEN, 22TH EDITION, 2022
"Knowledge and learning are at the foundation of our democracy, and that is reflected at the White House, where history comes to life."

The White House: An Historic Guide (Washington, D.C.: White House Historical Association, 2022), cover 3.

THE HISTORIC GUIDE WAS AN IMMEDIATE SUCCESS

WHEN THE WHITE HOUSE: AN HISTORIC GUIDE went on sale July 4, 1962, *My Thirty Years Backstairs at the White House,* by Lillian Rogers Parks, had been on the *New York Times Best Sellers List* for fifteen weeks. Also on the list were *To Kill a Mockingbird* by Harper Lee, and James Michener's *Hawaii*. As the White House gates opened to the public, hundreds of books were stacked optimistically behind a table set up at the very beginning of the route visitors would follow through the house.

Nash Castro, the Association's administrative officer, who joined other staffers to work the sales desk himself that first day, later described the scene:

I remember people coming in with grocery carts, if you can believe that. People came in with grocery carts and bought fifty or seventy-five or a hundred copies of the book. Now, don't ask me what they did with them because I didn't have time to ask.

The *Historic Guide* was an immediate success.

Marcia Mallet Anderson, "The White House: An Historic Guide Reaches Sixty Years in Print," *White House History Quarterly,* no. 60 (Winter 2021): 92.

PRINCIPAL ROOMS OF THE WHITE HOUSE

THE GROUND FLOOR

Ground Floor Corridor: Public tour visitors and most guests for social events enter the house itself from the East Wing by way of the Ground Floor Corridor. Lined with portraits of first ladies, the corridor is a "spine" of communication connecting all parts of the White House complex.

Diplomatic Reception Room: The formal entrance for visiting dignitaries and diplomats, the Diplomatic Reception Room is also the principal entrance for the first family and their personal guests.

China Room: Since 1918, the China Room has provided an exhibition space for examples of fine china, glassware, and silver used in the White House or owned by the first families.

Vermeil Room: The White House collection of gilded silver, or vermeil, gives its name to this room. Selections from the collection of more than 1,500 pieces are displayed here in two cabinets flanking the fireplace.

Library: Dedicated by President Franklin Delano Roosevelt to house books in 1935, the Library now holds approximately 2,700 volumes of primarily American history and literature.

THE WEST WING

Completed in 1902, the West Wing houses the offices of the president and president's staff.

Reception Room: After passing through security and entering the West Wing, visitors wait in the comfortably furnished Reception Room for their appointments.

Oval Office: One of the most symbolic spaces of the American presidency, the Oval Office was created in 1909 for President William Howard Taft. It was moved to its present location in 1934 by President Franklin D. Roosevelt.

Roosevelt Room: Just a few steps across the hall from the Oval Office, the Roosevelt Room is a conference room for the president.

Cabinet Room: Since 1902, the members of the president's cabinet—the vice president, the department heads, and additional officers with cabinet rank—have met in the Cabinet Room, a dedicated space near the Oval Office.

Press Room: Known officially as the James S. Brady Press Briefing Room, the Press Room has been regularly updated since it was established as a permanent space by President Richard Nixon in 1970. The room is often seen on

PRINCIPAL ROOMS OF THE WHITE HOUSE

television news broadcasts as the president or the president's press secretary addresses and responds to news reporters, who fill the seats.

East Garden Room: Also known as the Bookseller's Area, the East Garden Room is used by the White House Historical Association to sell the White House guidebook and other educational resources during public tours.

THE EAST WING

Providing a social entrance to the White House, the East Wing as we know it today was built in 1942, replacing a smaller 1902 structure built on the site of the original 1805 wing. The public tour begins here as visitors enter into the wood-paneled East Lobby. This wing houses the Office of the First Lady, the White House Visitors Office, the White House Military Office, and the Calligraphy Office.

East Colonnade is an enclosed passage linking the East Wing to the Ground Floor Corridor of the Residence.

Movie Theater: Accessible from the East Colonnade, the Movie Theater was first created for use as a cloakroom during the Theodore Roosevelt presidency. In 1942, when President Franklin D. Roosevelt expanded the East Wing, he converted the cloakroom into the Movie Theater. Its long, narrow proportions are ideal for viewing films.

THE STATE FLOOR

Situated between the East and West Wings, the Residence is the central structure of the White House and holds the first family's private living spaces on the Second and Third Floors as well as historic public spaces on the Ground Floor and State Floor.

State Floor Entrance Hall: The marble-tiled Entrance Hall is the formal entrance to the White House.

Cross Hall: Uniting the State Rooms, with the East Room and State Dining Room at opposite ends and the Green, Blue, and Red Rooms on the south side, the Cross Hall is a primary passageway as well as a gallery of portraits of recent presidents.

Grand Staircase: The formal connection between the Second Floor Private Quarters and the State Floor, the Grand Staircase is used by the president to make formal entrances during special events.

East Room: The great ceremonial room of the White House, the East Room is, at 85 by 40 feet, the largest

PRINCIPAL ROOMS
OF THE WHITE HOUSE

room in the house, extending the full length of the building, north to south.

Green Room: The first of the State Rooms to be named for the color of its textiles, the Green Room provides a serene setting for small gatherings, interviews, teas, and social activities.

Blue Room: Distinguished by its central location, elegant oval shape, and striking vista through the South Portico, the Blue Room is often used for receptions, and, during the holiday season, the official White House Christmas tree stands in its center.

Red Room: A richly formal setting for teas, small receptions, and meetings, the Red Room has been decorated in red since 1845.

State Dining Room: The setting for many State Dinners—when a head of state is entertained, as well as for many official dinners—when the guest of honor is a prime minister, ambassador, or private citizen—the State Dining Room is the second largest room in the White House.

THE SECOND FLOOR

Yellow Oval Room: The most formal room on the Second Floor, the Yellow Oval Room provides access to the Truman Balcony, overlooking the South Lawn. It provides a comfortable sitting room for the first family, and is used by the president to greet guests of honor before State Dinners.

Lincoln Bedroom: Once used as an office and cabinet room by President Abraham Lincoln, the Lincoln Bedroom and the adjacent Lincoln Sitting Room are used for personal guests of the president's family, as well as for official guests.

Queens' Bedroom: With its adjacent sitting room, the Queens' Bedroom has served as one of two principal guest suites for distinguished visitors since 1902. It is named for the visiting royalty who have slept here, including the queens of Great Britain, Greece, the Netherlands, Norway, and Spain.

BIRTHPLACES OF THE PRESIDENTS BY STATE.

CA 1

HI 1

VIRGINIA
George Washington
Thomas Jefferson
James Madison
James Monroe
William Henry
  Harrison
John Tyler
Zachary Taylor
Woodrow Wilson

OHIO
Ulysses S. Grant
Rutherford B. Hayes
James A. Garfield
Benjamin Harrison
William McKinley
William H. Taft
Warren G. Harding

NEW YORK
Martin Van Buren
Millard Fillmore
Theodore Roosevelt
Franklin Roosevelt
Donald J. Trump

MASSACHUSETTS
John Adams
John Quincy Adams
John F. Kennedy
George H. W. Bush

NORTH CAROLINA
James K. Polk
Andrew Johnson

PENNSYLVANIA
James Buchanan
Joe Biden

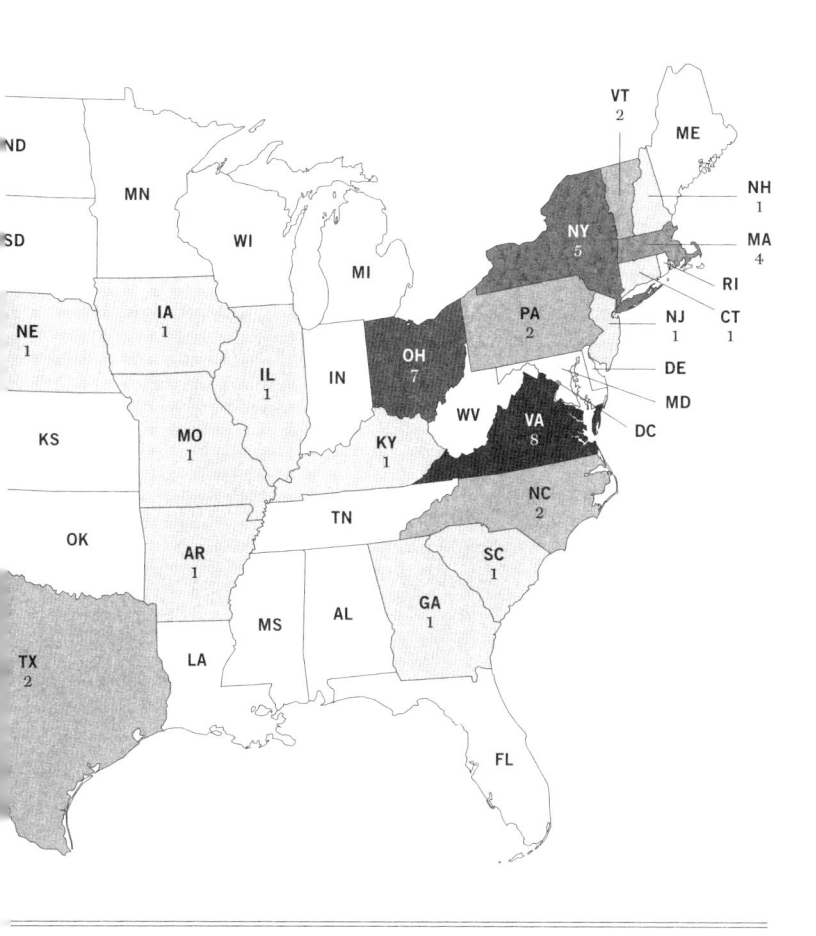

TEXAS	CALIFORNIA	ILLINOIS	NEBRASKA
Dwight D. Eisenhower	Richard Nixon	Ronald Reagan	Gerald Ford
Lyndon B. Johnson	CONNECTICUT	IOWA	NEW HAMPSHIRE
	George W. Bush	Herbert Hoover	Franklin Pierce
VERMONT			
Chester A. Arthur	GEORGIA	KENTUCKY	NEW JERSEY
Calvin Coolidge	Jimmy Carter	Abraham Lincoln	Grover Cleveland
ARKANSAS	HAWAII	MISSOURI	SOUTH CAROLINA
Bill Clinton	Barack Obama	Harry S. Truman	Andrew Jackson

THE PEOPLE'S HOUSE MISCELLANY

THE OFFICIAL PORTRAIT COLLECTION

PORTRAITIST	PORTRAIT	YEAR
Herbert E. Abrams	Jimmy Carter	1982
	George H. W. Bush	1994
Eliphalet F. Andrews	Martha Washington	1878
	Andrew Johnson	1880
Francesco Anelli	Julia Tyler	1846–48
George Augusta	Rosalynn Carter	1984
John Henry Brown	James Buchanan	1851
Richard M. Brown	Lou Henry Hoover	1950
Joseph H. Bush	Zachary Taylor	1848
Douglas Granville Chandor	Eleanor Roosevelt	1949
Théobald Chartran	Edith Roosevelt	1902
Howard Chandler Christy	Grace Coolidge	1924
F. Graham Cootes	Woodrow Wilson	1936
Calvin Curtis	James A. Garfield	1881
Felix DeCossio	Betty Ford	1977
Ralph E. W. Earl	Emily Donelson	1830
	Andrew Jackson	1835
Charles A. Fagan	Barbara Bush	2005
Byrd Farioletti	Eliza Johnson	1961
Elmer W. Greene	Herbert Hoover	1956
George P. A. Healy	Millard Fillmore	1857
	John Quincy Adams	1858
	Martin Van Buren	1858
	James K. Polk	1858
	Franklin Pierce	1858
	John Tyler	1859
	Abraham Lincoln	1869
Katherine Helm	Mary Todd Lincoln	1925
Charles S. Hopkinson	Calvin Coolidge	1932
Daniel Huntington	Lucy Hayes	1881
	Rutherford B. Hayes	1884
	Chester A. Arthur	1885
	Caroline Harrison	1894
Henry Inman	Angelica Van Buren	1842
Eastman Johnson	Grover Cleveland	1891
	Benjamin Harrison	1895
Martha Greta Kempton	Bess Truman	1967
	Harry S. Truman	1947

THE OFFICIAL PORTRAIT COLLECTION

PORTRAITIST	PORTRAIT	YEAR

Everett Raymond Kinstler .... *Gerald Ford* 1977
                                    Ronald Reagan 1991
Simmie Knox .... *Hillary Rodham Clinton* 2003
                                    William J. Clinton 2002
Bror Kronstrand.................. *Helen Herron Taft*................. 1910
James Reid Lambdin............... *William Henry Harrison*........... 1835
Philip de László .... *Florence Kling Harding*............ 1921
Robert McCurdy.................. *Barack Obama* 2022
Samuel F. B. Morse .... *James Monroe* 1819
Adolfo Muller-Ury................ *Edith Bolling Wilson* 1916
Harriet Anderson Stubbs Murphy ... *William McKinley* 1902
Rembrandt Peale .... *Thomas Jefferson* 1800
Frank O. Salisbury................. *Franklin D. Roosevelt*............... 1947
John Howard Sanden .... *Laura Bush* 2012
                                    George W. Bush 2011
John Singer Sargent................ *Theodore Roosevelt* 1903
Sharon Sprung .... *Michelle Obama* 2022
Aaron Shikler .... *Jacqueline Kennedy* 1970
                                    John F. Kennedy 1970
                                    Nancy Reagan 1987
                                    Ronald Reagan 1989
Elizabeth Shoumatoff .... *Lady Bird Johnson* 1968
                                    Lyndon B. Johnson................. 1968
E. Hodgson Smart .... *Warren G. Harding*................ 1923
Casimir Gregory Stapko .... *Frances Cleveland*.................. 1952
Thomas E. Stephens .... *Mamie Eisenhower*................. 1959
Gilbert Stuart .... *George Washington*................ 1797
                                    Dolley Madison..................... 1804
                                    Louisa Adams 1821–26
Emily Drayton Taylor .... *Ida McKinley*...................... 1899
John Trumbull .... *John Adams*..................... 1792–93
Henry Ulke .... *Ulysses S. Grant* 1875
John Vanderlyn................... *James Madison* 1816
J. Anthony Wills .... *Dwight D. Eisenhower* 1967
                                    Richard M. Nixon.................. 1984
Henriette Wyeth.................. *Pat Nixon*........................ 1978
Anders L. Zorn .... *William H. Taft*..................... 1911

THE *RESOLUTE* DESK

---- PARTNER'S DESK ----

William Evenden, Royal Naval Dockyard at Chatham, England, probably from a design by Morant, Boyd & Blanford, London, 1880

Kneehole panel by Rudolph Bauss
Washington, D.C., 1945

White oak, mahogany / white oak, teak
29 × 72 × 48 in. (73.7 × 182.9 × 121.9 cm)

Gift of Queen Victoria, 1880

MARKS:
Underside on all of the exterior drawer fronts—stamped "MORANT BOYD & BLANFORD / 91 NEW BOND STREET"; lock plates—stamped company armorial mark "BY ROYAL / LETTERS PATENT / FOUR LEVERS / SAFETY LOCK / COMYN CHINC & Co."

INSCRIPTIONS:
On brass plaque located on center drawer above kneehole: "H.M.S. 'Resolute', forming part of the expedition sent in search of Sir John Franklin in 1852, was abandoned in Latitude 74°41' N. Longitude 101°22' W. on 15th May 1854. She was discovered and extricated in September

78 THE PEOPLE'S HOUSE MISCELLANY

THE *RESOLUTE* DESK

1855, in Latitude 67° N. by Captain Buddington of the United States Whaler 'George Henry.' The ship was purchased, fitted out and sent to England, as a gift to Her Majesty Queen Victoria by the President and People of the United States, as a token of goodwill & friendship. This table was made from her timbers when she was broken up, and is presented by the Queen of Great Britain & Ireland, to the President of the United States, as a memorial of the courtesy and loving kindness which dictated the offer of the gift of the 'Resolute.'"

NOTES:

Called the "*Resolute* Desk," this double-pedestal desk was made from the oak timbers of the British ship HMS *Resolute* as a gift to President Rutherford B. Hayes from Queen Victoria in 1880. The desk was used in the president's office on the Second Floor of the Residence, 1880–1902, and in the president's study, 1902–48.

In 1945, a panel carved with the Presidential Coat of Arms was installed under President Harry S. Truman, just before the executive order that mandated that the eagle's head face the olive branch.

Used in the Broadcast Room on the Ground Floor, 1952–61, it was first used in the Oval Office by President John F. Kennedy, 1961–63. On off-site exhibit tours, 1964–77, it has been used again in the Oval Office 1977–89 (Carter, Reagan) and 1993–present (Clinton, Bush, Obama, Trump, Biden, Trump).

A proposal for the desk, not as actually executed, was depicted in *Frank Leslie's Illustrated Newspaper* in 1880, while a description from the *Chatham News* reported that it was made by William Evenden, "a skilled wood carver and joiner, employed in Chatham Dockyard." Another desk was made from the timbers for the wife of American merchant Henry Grinnell, who financed two expeditions to search for John Franklin (Whaling Museum, New Bedford, Mass.).

Betty C. Monkman et al. *Furnishing the White House: The Decorative Arts Collection* (Washington, D.C.: White House Historical Association, 2023), 358.

PIERRE-ANTOINE BELLANGÉ PIER TABLE

PIER TABLE

Pierre-Antoine Bellangé (1758–1827), Paris, c. 1817
Gilded beechwood, marble, mirror glass
U.S. Government purchase for the President's House, 1817

"1 Gilded wood console of 5 feet 10 inches long by 3 feet 4 inches high, double baluster legs, rear pilasters, a large mirror frame, carved and gilded" with the mirror glass and "1 white marble [top] of 5 feet 10 by 22 inches" totaling 715.40 francs.

From a 53-piece suite purchased in 1817 for "the large oval room," this is the only piece to have remained continuously in the White House Collection.

Betty C. Monkman et al. *Furnishing the White House: The Decorative Arts Collection* (Washington, D.C.: White House Historical Association, 2023), 345.

THE TREATY TABLE

CONFERENCE TABLE
Pottier & Stymus Manufacturing Co., New York, 1869
Walnut / mahogany, tulip poplar; leather
U.S. Government purchase for the President's House, 1869

One "table for 8 persons" from a suite of furniture purchased for the cabinet room in 1869. Eight locking drawers were available to the president and the seven cabinet officers as of 1869 (State, War, Treasury, Navy, Interior, Attorney General, and Postmaster General). The table continued to be used by the cabinet until 1902. In 1961, First Lady Jacqueline Kennedy reassembled the surviving pieces from the suite, including this table, in that same Second Floor room, renamed the Treaty Room, that had served as the cabinet room from 1865 to 1902. Among the historic documents that have been signed on this table are:

1. The Peace Protocol ending hostilities of the Spanish-American War, August 12, 1898, witnessed by President William McKinley in the cabinet room.

2. The Pact of Paris (Kellogg-Briand Peace Pact), 1929, signed by President Calvin Coolidge in the East Room.

3. Arms and nuclear testing treaties with the Soviet Union signed in the East Room by Gerald Ford (1976), Ronald Reagan (1987), and George H. W. Bush (1990).

4. Treaties with former Soviet republics (Russia, Ukraine, Kazakhstan), 1992, signed by President George H. W. Bush in the East Room.

5. Middle East peace documents including: Egyptian-Israeli Peace Treaty, 1979, on the North Lawn, witnessed by Prident Jimmy Carter; and The Israel-Palestinian Declaration of Principles, 1993, on the South Lawn, hosted by President Bill Clinton.

Betty C. Monkman et al. *Furnishing the White House: The Decorative Arts Collection* (Washington, D.C.: White House Historical Association, 2023), 356.

THE PRESIDENTS AND BASEBALL

FOR MORE THAN A CENTURY, the relationship between presidents and the national pastime has been wound as tightly as a new baseball. Most fans are familiar with the ceremonial first pitch, which was a longtime Washington tradition, even with a thirty-three-year absence. But presidents have played other, more substantive roles, working behind the scenes to keep the sport going during wartime and even trying to find a new team for Washington, D.C.

From William Howard Taft to Richard Nixon, every president made at least one opening-day toss in Washington, which usually started its season a day early in what was known as the presidential opener. Congress recessed for the afternoon so members could attend. And unlike today, when presidents throw from the pitcher's mound, for most of the twentieth century they tossed the ball from the stands, over a scrum of photographers onto the field into a crowd of players from both teams, who would battle for it, with the winning player getting an autograph from the chief executive.

When Taft made his opening-day toss in 1910, baseball was the only team sport that mattered in the United States. Football has since eclipsed it as the nation's most popular sport, but nothing matches baseball's hold on American culture.

Fred Frommer, "The Presidents and Baseball: Presidential Openers and Other Traditions," *White House History Quarterly*, no. 55 (Fall 2019): 6–19.

THE PRESIDENTS AND BASEBALL

APRIL 14, 1910
William Howard Taft threw the opening toss at the first home game of the Washington Senators, becoming the first sitting U.S. president to throw out the first ball at a major league baseball game.

JULY 7, 1937
Franklin Roosevelt became the first president to attend an All-Star Game—only the fifth one in history—on July 7, 1937.... He waved his hat to cheering fans as his convertible made its way down the field, past a procession of lined up players.

SEPTEMBER 8, 1945
During World War II the presidential opening-day tradition was suspended, but Harry S. Truman made a point of throwing out the first toss on September 8, 1945, just six days after Japan's surrender was formalized.

APRIL 14 AND 16, 1953
Dwight D. Eisenhower angered some baseball fans his first year as president when he decided to go golfing in Augusta, Georgia, rather than throw out the Washington Senators opening-day toss on April 14, 1953. But the game was rained out, and he flew back and threw the toss at the rescheduled opener on April 16. He stayed for just one and one-half innings before flying back to his golfing trip.

APRIL 14, 2005
President George W. Bush threw out the ceremonial first pitch on the Nationals opening day in 2005. The occasion marked baseball's return to Washington, D.C., after a thirty-three-year absence.

Fred Frommer, "The Presidents and Baseball: Presidential Openers and Other Traditions," *White House History Quarterly*, no. 55 (Fall 2019): 6–19.

THEODORE ROOSEVELT ON JUJITSU

WRITING TO HIS SON Kermit in February 1905, President Theodore Roosevelt described a jujitsu lesson in the East Room: "I still box with [Joseph] Grant, who has now become the champion middle-weight wrestler of the United States. Yesterday afternoon we had Professor Yamashita [Yoshiaki] up here to wrestle with Grant. It was very interesting, but of course jujitsu . . . is really meant for practice in killing or disabling our adversary. In consequence, Grant did not know what to do except to put Yamashita on his back, and Yamashita was perfectly content to be on his back. Inside of a minute Yamashita had choked Grant, and inside of two minutes more he got an elbow hold on him that would have enabled him to break his arm; so that there is no question but that he could have put Grant out. So far this made it evident that the jujitsu man could handle the ordinary wrestler. But Grant, in the actual wrestling and throwing was about as good as the Japanese, and he was so much stronger that he evidently hurt and wore out the Japanese."

William Seale, "The Long Shadow of Jiujitsu in the East Room: President Theodore Roosevelt Learns Self-Defense," *White House History Quarterly*, no. 55 (Fall 2019): 64, quoting Theodore Roosevelt to Kermit Roosevelt, February 24, 1905, in *Theodore Roosevelt's Letters to His Children* (New York: C. Scribner's Sons, 1919): 116–17. Illustration by John Hutton.

THE OFFICIAL RULES OF HOOVER BALL, A WHITE HOUSE RITUAL FOR PRESIDENT HERBERT HOOVER

THE OFFICIAL COURT IS 66 by 30 feet. The ball is to weigh 4 to 6 pounds. This contrasts with a volleyball, which weighs less than 10 ounces. The Hoover Ball consists of a hand-stitched leather cover around a sandbag core wrapped in cotton batting. The net is to be 8 feet high. Teams consist of two to four players. Scoring is exactly like tennis: love, 15, 30, 40 (deuce, ad-in, ad-out), game. Teams play matches of best of five or seven games. Points are scored when a team fails to catch the ball, fails to return the ball across the net, returns the ball out-of-bounds, or fails to return the ball to the proper court area. Points in question are played over. Good sportsmanship is expected. The ball is served from the back line. The serve is rotated among one team until the game is won. Teams alternate serving after each game. Teams change courts after every two games. The ball must be caught on the fly and returned from the point it was caught. There is no running with the ball or passing to teammates. Each team's court is divided in half, with the mid-court line part of the front court. A ball caught in the front half of the court must be returned to the back half of the opponent's court. This prevents spiking. If the ball does not reach the back court, the opponent wins the point. Balls caught must be played. A player who is carried out-of-bounds by the force of the ball may return in-bounds before the return. A ball that hits the out-of-bounds line is considered in-bounds. A ball that hits the net on the way over is a live ball but if thrown from the front court must reach the opponent's back court to be good. Teams may substitute freely at dead ball situations.

Quoted in Matthew Schaefer, "Hoover Ball and Wellness in the White House," *White House History Quarterly*, no. 55 (Fall 2019): 51. The Hoover Ball pictured above is preserved in the collection of the Herbert Hoover Presidential Library.

THE OFFICIAL STATE VISITS OF QUEEN ELIZABETH II

QUEEN ELIZABETH II met every American president from Harry S. Truman to Donald J. Trump, with the exception of Lyndon B. Johnson. Her official visits to the United States included:

1951
First official visit to Washington, D.C.
As Princess Elizabeth, she was hosted by President Harry S. Truman.

1957
State Visit hosted by President Dwight D. Eisenhower on the occasion of the 350th anniversary of the establishment of the first permanent English settlement at Jamestown in Virginia.

1976
State Visit hosted by President Gerald R. Ford on the occasion of the U.S. Bicentennial.

1983
State Dinner in her honor hosted by President and Mrs. Ronald Reagan at the M. H. de Young Memorial Museum in San Francisco.

1991
State Visit hosted by President George H. W. Bush.

2007
State Visit hosted by President George W. Bush on the occasion of the 400th anniversary of the establishment of the first permanent English settlement at Jamestown in Virginia.

Drawn from "Queen Elizabeth II: The Royal Visits," *White House History Quarterly*, no. 64 (Winter 2022): entire issue.

PAPAL VISITS TO THE WHITE HOUSE

THERE HAVE BEEN ONLY three visits by the pope to the White House:

October 6, 1979
Pope John Paul II

April 16, 2008
Pope Benedict XVI

September 23, 2015
Pope Francis

The White House staff remembers:

"I was also here for the only three visits the pope has made to the White House: Pope John Paul II in 1979, Pope Benedict XVI in 2008, and Pope Francis in 2015. Knowing that yellow and white are the official colors of the papacy, we used yellow flowers in place of the usual red on the South Portico for Pope Francis's Arrival Ceremony."—Dale Haney

The visits of religious leaders such as Popes John Paul II, Benedict XVI, and Francis are also rare enough that invitations to the welcome ceremonies are highly sought after. "My phone rang off the hook," said [aide to Rosalynn Carter] Mary Finch Hoyt of the run-up to the 1979 visit of Pope John Paul II. "I never knew I had so many Catholic friends." Twenty-nine years later as many as 13,000 people stood on the South Lawn to welcome Pope Benedict in 2008. Benedict's visit coincided with his eighty-first birthday so after the formal Arrival Ceremony, the crowd sang "Happy Birthday" and the White House chef presented him with a tiered cake frosted in the Vatican colors. In 2015, almost 15,000 people gathered on the South Lawn to greet Pope Francis.

Quoted in Marcia Mallet Anderson with Dale Haney, "Fifty Years Devoted to the White House Gardens and Grounds: The Career of Dale Haney, Superintendent of the White House Grounds," *White House History Quarterly*, no. 65 (Spring 2022): 10.

Mary Jo Binker "The White House Social Secretary: Collected Reflections," *White House History*, no. 49 (Spring 2018): 26.

THE PRESIDENTIAL TURKEY PARDON

BENJAMIN FRANKLIN proposed the turkey as the national symbol, but the eagle won out. The turkey, however, was not forgotten and made its appearance later on as the symbol of Thanksgiving. The story of the Thanksgiving turkeys at the White House—whether landing on the dinner table or pardoned—has been a highly publicized annual ritual since the presidency of Ulysses S. Grant. Today a presidential "pardon" for the otherwise doomed bird lightens the political mood and, at Thanksgiving, signals the start of the long American holiday season. President Abraham Lincoln's clemency to a turkey in 1863, due to the pleas of his son Tad, may well have been the origin for the pardoning ceremony. However, throughout the nineteenth and much of the twentieth century, turkeys were sent to the president and his family as gifts and became the centerpiece of Thanksgiving dinner. The gifts reflected the regional pride of the poultry producers and a desire to promote their product.

With the emergence of an organized national poultry industry by the mid-twentieth century, it was logical that a White House stage would be sought to showcase and to publicize the consumption of turkeys over the holidays.

Mythmakers also cite the presentation of a turkey during a ceremony at the White House on December 15, 1947, as the origin of the turkey pardon. The National Turkey Federation and the Poultry and Egg National Board, the organizations most active in promoting the industry, presented the president with the turkey, an event that did become a major photo opportunity and reprieve, if not a pardon.

William Bushong, "The Story of the Thanksgiving Turkey at the White House," *White House History*, no. 43 (Fall 2016): 46–57.

THE MATTER OF RATS IN THE WHITE HOUSE

PRESIDENT JIMMY CARTER wrote in his memoir, *White House Diary*, "For two or three months now I've been telling them to get rid of the mice. They still seem to be growing in numbers, and I am determined either to fire somebody or get the mice cleared out—or both." Thanks to President Carter's orders, prevention developed over time and is fairly well in hand today.

The General Services Administration is tasked with it and uses private extermination companies, as does the National Park Service, which maintains some of the buildings of the White House complex and all the grounds. The road has not always been sunny. One day Barbara Bush, who as first lady swam a mile a day when possible, was in the White House swimming pool outside the West Wing stroking along, when into her view, through her swimming mask, appeared a rat: "He did not look like a Walt Disney friend, I'll tell you that," she told a reporter, "it was enormous." President George H. W. Bush, nearby, came to the rescue.

Rats and mice are thus an ongoing story at the White House. Held at bay for now, one can only assume that the White House will hear from them again.

Excerpted from William Seale, "The Matter of Rats in the White House," *White House History*, no. 43 (Fall 2016): 66–72. Illustration by John Hutton.

DOGS AND CATS

Presidents whose White House households included	Presidents whose White House households included
DOGS	CATS
John Adams	*Abraham Lincoln*
Andrew Jackson	*Rutherford B. Hayes*
Franklin Pierce	*Theodore Roosevelt*
James Buchanan	*Woodrow Wilson*
Abraham Lincoln	*Calvin Coolidge*
Ulysses S. Grant	*Herbert Hoover*
Rutherford B. Hayes	*John F. Kennedy*
James Garfield	*Gerald Ford*
Grover Cleveland	*Jimmy Carter*
Benjamin Harrison	*Bill Clinton*
Woodrow Wilson	*George W. Bush*
Warren Harding	*Joe Biden*
Calvin Coolidge	
Herbert Hoover	
Franklin D. Roosevelt	
Harry Truman	
John F. Kennedy	
Richard Nixon	
Gerald Ford	
Jimmy Carter	
Ronald Reagan	
George H. W. Bush	
Bill Clinton	
George W. Bush	
Barack Obama	
Joe Biden	

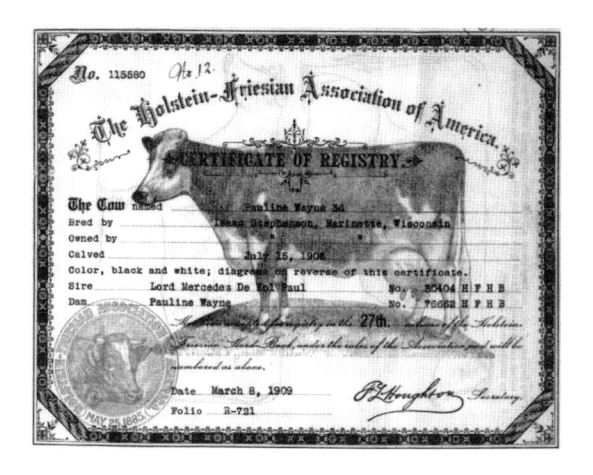

PAULINE WAYNE III
THE MOST FAMOUS COW IN AMERICA

CALVED:	*July 15, 1906*
BIRTHPLACE:	*Isaac Stephenson's Farm, Kenosha, Wisconsin*
REGISTERED:	*No. 115580 by the Holstein-Friesian Association*
SIRE (father):	*Lord Mercedes De Kol Paul*
DAM (mother):	*Pauline Wayne*
SON:	*Big Bill*
GIVEN TO:	*President William Howard Taft*
ACCOMMODATIONS:	*White House Executive Stables*
GREAT ADVENTURE:	*1911 trip to the International Dairy Show, Milwaukee*
PRODUCTIVITY:	*9 gallons of milk per day by age four*
MEDIA COVERAGE:	*More than 5,000 print stories from 1910 to 1913*
REPORTED LIKES:	*Chewing on her cud, massages, being left alone*
REPORTED DISLIKES:	*Photographers, reporters*
RETIRED:	*To Isaac Stephenson's farm, 1913.*

Jonathan Pliska, "Pauline Wayne III: The Most Famous Cow in America," *White House History Quarterly*, no. 76 (Winter 2025): 36–47.

BORN THE SAME YEAR

ULYSSES S. GRANT.

RUTHERFORD B. HAYES

---1767---
John Quincy Adams
Andrew Jackson

---1822---
Ulysses S. Grant
Rutherford B. Hayes

---1913---
Richard M. Nixon
Gerald R. Ford

---1924---
Jimmy Carter
George H. W. Bush

---1946---
George W. Bush
Bill Clinton
Donald J. Trump

DIED THE SAME DAY

THOMAS JEFFERSON

————— JULY 4, 1826 —————
John Adams
Thomas Jefferson

THE PEOPLE'S HOUSE MISCELLANY

YELLOW: A SYMBOL OF LIGHT AND OPTIMISM

FIRST LADY LADY BIRD JOHNSON often chose to wear bright yellow for both formal events and public appearances. She considered yellow a symbol of light and optimism.

Mrs. Johnson wore a yellow gown for her official portrait by Elizabeth Shoumatoff, 1968

a yellow coat to the Arrival Ceremony for President Alfredo Stroessner of Paraguay, 1968

a yellow Adele Simpson dress to say good-bye to daughter Luci and Patrick Nugent as they left for their honeymoon, following a White House wedding reception, 1966

a John Moore fur-trimmed canary-yellow Inaugural Ball ensemble, 1966

a yellow Mollie Parnis dress and scarf to read to children at a Project Head Start program, 1968

Kimberly Chrisman-Campbell "Seduced by Style: Lady Bird Johnson's White House Fashion," *White House History Quarterly*, no. 66 (Summer 2022), 22–37.

RED: A PICKER-UPPER

FIRST LADY NANCY REAGAN'S STYLE will forever be associated with the color red, which she explained was a "picker-upper." Red for every occasion, rain or shine, could be found in her wardrobe.

Mrs. Reagan wore a red Galanos gown for her official portrait by Aaron Shikler, 1987

a bright red raincoat to welcome Prince Philip and Queen Elizabeth II to California, 1985

a red sweater and blouse to welcome President Reagan back home to the White House from the hospital following an assassination attempt, 1981

a red gown by Oscar de la Renta for a State Dinner in honor of British Prime Minister Margaret Thatcher, 1988

a red gown by Valentino for a White House State Dinner in honor of Japanese Crown Prince Akihito and his wife Crown Princess Michiko, 1987

Rebecca Durgin Kerr "From Hollywood to the White House: Nancy Reagan's Style," *White House History Quarterly*, no. 66 (Summer 2022), 38–53.

WHITE HOUSE HISTORY CONTINUES TO BE MADE

THE WHITE HOUSE HISTORY, fun facts, and things to know listed on the previous pages change frequently. The lists provided here are current as of May 2025 but will change each time

... a new president is elected

... a president throws a first pitch

... a State Dinner honors a head of state

... a Christmas tree is displayed in the Blue Room

... an Official White House Christmas Ornament is released

... a pet joins the first family

... a first family member marries at the White House

... an official portrait is added to the White House Collection

... children are welcomed to the White House Easter Egg Roll

... a White House tradition begins.